Education in
the Armed Forces

Education in
the Armed Forces

JAMES C. SHELBURNE

Educational Advisor
Air University
Maxwell Air Force Base

KENNETH J. GROVES

Director of Evaluation
and Special Studies
Air University
Maxwell Air Force Base

The Center for Applied Research in Education, Inc.
New York

Foreword

Education in the Armed Forces is a timely
and informed treatise on programs which have more actual and potential impact on our society than is generally recognized.

The authors, Dr. James C. Shelburne and Dr. Kenneth J. Groves,
as Educational Advisor and Director of Evaluation, respectively,
of Air University, have an unexcelled vantage point for describing
and interpreting education in the Air Force, and for studying educational programs in other branches of the Armed Forces. They
have made good use of their opportunities and have capitalized also
on their previous experiences and their broad training in education
and psychology.

The importance of this study may be gauged partly by the magnitude of the programs described. As the authors note, the Armed
Forces are operating what is probably the largest adult education
program in the country—a program which enrolls close to 400,000
men annually. Of greater significance is the fact that these educational programs affect practically all young men, including many
who drop out before completing high school. The effects will be
even greater if President Johnson's recent directive to provide training for those now barred from induction because of illiteracy or
mental retardation becomes established policy.

The training in the Armed Forces obviously is focused on military objectives. These objectives, however, demand education and
training of great breadth because men in the services must be competent to perform a wide variety of tasks and to adapt to many
types of contingency, although most of these may not be encoun-
tered during the tour of duty. The training aims to provide not only
the technical knowledge and skill essential to proficiency with present weapon systems, but also the technological understanding adequate to the mastery of new systems and techniques.

Because of such considerations, education in the Armed Forces seeks outcomes which often are relevant for civilian occupations, and for an understanding of our own and other societies. The Department of Defense serves, therefore, as an important training establishment for industry and for civilian life. This is nonetheless true in those cases where the objectives and the outcome of training may relate negatively to values and behaviors for effective living outside the military forces.

It will be well if *Education in the Armed Forces* alerts the American public to the consequences for national life of this extensive program of education and training; it will be even better if it leads to continuing critical examination of the objectives, content, and methods of training by qualified educators and other thoughtful persons outside, as well as inside, the Defense Department. Perhaps this largely descriptive report will be followed by others more analytical in nature.

I commend the authors for opening up an important field for public scrutiny and for further inquiry.

FRANCIS S. CHASE
Dean, Graduate School of Education
University of Chicago

Education in the Armed Forces

James C. Shelburne
Kenneth J. Groves

Few Americans are aware of the nature and scope of one of the largest educational programs in the country. All who have been in military service during the past 20 years have had more or less experience with this educational system, probably without realizing fully its vast extent and the tremendous effort that is put into this phase of the nation's military operations. Few taxpayers are aware of the precise uses to which their federal taxes are put in the maintenance of national defense, particularly the very large share of the more than $50 billions of the defense budget that is devoted to education and training. A description of this expensive, expansive, and most effective educational system is the purpose of this volume by Shelburne and Groves.

In the Library of Education most of the volumes are devoted to various phases or features of what is usually considered "the" system of education in the United States—the primary and elementary schools, the secondary schools, and the colleges and universities. The volume by Shelburne and Groves, by contrast, treats a publicly supported and controlled educational system that is supplemental to, built upon, and only loosely coordinated with the regular system of public and private elementary and high schools and colleges and universities. Some of the aspects of education in the armed forces are closely related to what is usually known as adult education; other parts of the military educational system are very similar in nature to the formally organized schools at the secondary, college, graduate, and even post-doctoral levels. Curiously, too, here is a system of public education in the American democracy that is completely under federal control—a characterization that will immediately raise the hackles of a good many educators and other thoughtful citizens, who are convinced that "federal control" and "good education" are completely contradictory.

The volume should perhaps be of greatest use to high school and college counselors, who have strategic opportunities to advise young men and women about to enter military service. It would seem especially important to give those entering military service a keen appreciation of the broad educational opportunity that awaits them there. One who can look upon his military service as a continuation of his education—not just an interruption in it, or a postponement of his plans for civilian life—is likely to improve greatly both the pleasure and the profit that may be gained from experience in the armed forces. Particularly to be stressed are the opportunities to obtain training useful upon return to civilian life, and the off-duty educational programs, in which attainment may be converted directly into credits and other forms of progress toward academic diplomas and degrees.

Besides its usefulness to counselors, almost any educator should be able to profit by the intensive look, provided in this volume, at a perhaps unfamiliar educational system. Finally, any citizen interested in the welfare of the country should know the facts about the educational programs in the armed forces. A reading of this volume by Shelburne and Groves should do much to instill confidence that the defense of the country by the armed forces is being intelligently handled through a sound program of education for the military personnel.

JOHN DALE RUSSELL
Content Editor

Contents

CHAPTER I

Background

Whatever arguments may be drawn from particular examples, su-
perficially viewed, a thorough examination of the subject will evince
that the Art of War is both comprehensive and complicated; that it
demands much previous study, that the possession of it in its most
approved and perfect state is always of great moment to the security
of a Nation.
George Washington, *Eighth Annual Address,* (December 7, 1796)

Although a wealth of material has been published in books, periodicals, government documents, and various reports dealing with
aspects of training and education in the Armed Forces, comparatively few recent treatments have been written on the subject as a
whole.[1] Within the past three decades, a near-revolution has taken
place in warfare, in weapon technology, and in the means for
weapon delivery. These and other factors have had their impact on
education in the military establishment.

This monograph has a twofold purpose: to indicate the dimensions of the military training and educational task in the Armed
Forces of the United States, and to identify and discuss the various
categories of the task. Throughout this discussion, the concern is
with the active-duty forces. The comparable programs for the Reserve components, including the National Guard, and for civil defense are not identified as such and are not included.

Introduction

The fortunes of war and the evolution of Western civilization and
of weapon technology have combined to catapult the United States
into a position of leadership which it did not seek and for which, in
some respects, it was not prepared. Its military commitments sur-
pass those of any of its allies and probably those of the Soviet Union.
These commitments are worldwide and at present include treaties

---

[1] North Callahan, *The Armed Forces as a Career* (New York: McGraw-Hill
Book Company, 1947); Harold F. Clark and Harold S. Sloan, *Classrooms in the
Military* (New York: Teachers College, Bureau of Publications, Columbia Uni-
versity, 1964).

1

with some forty nations and military assistance pacts with others. It has pledged support to regional organizations such as the North American Treaty Organization (NATO), the Southeast Asia Treaty Organization (SEATO), the Organization of American States (OAS), and the Australia-New Zealand-United States Treaty (ANZUS). Though not a member, it participates with member countries in the Central Treaty Organization (CENTO) growing out of the Baghdad Pact, and has bilateral treaties with the Philippines, Japan, South Korea, and the Republic of China.

The United States military force required to meet these obligations approximates 2.75 million men and women in uniform and over a million civilians. Almost 0.75 million military personnel are deployed overseas in the Caribbean, the Azores, Morocco, Spain, France, the United Kingdom, Iceland, West Germany (including West Berlin), Italy, Libya, the Mediterranean, Turkey, Thailand, South Vietnam, the Philippines, Okinawa, South Korea, Japan, Hawaii, Alaska, and with the fleets in the Atlantic and Pacific.[2]

Another way of looking at the dimensions of the military task is from the point of view of cost. Over fifty cents of every tax dollar is spent for national defense. For the fiscal year 1964—that is, the period beginning July 1, 1963, and ending June 30, 1964—the funds considered necessary for training and education in the Armed

TABLE 1

INDIVIDUAL TRAINING AND EDUCATION:
OBLIGATIONAL AUTHORITY

	1962 (in millions)	1963 (in millions)	1964 (in millions)
Recruit training	$ 623	$ 599	$ 712
Technical training	998	1010	1056
Professional training	214	224	223
Flight training	632	639	726
Other *	386	376	374
	$2853	$2848	$3091

Source: The Office of the Assistant Secretary of Defense (Manpower), in a letter dated April 17, 1963.

* Includes funds for three service academies, general training devices, films, publications, testing activities, correspondence schools, and miscellaneous training support activities as well as the operating costs of the major training command headquarters within each service.

[2] *Department of Defense Annual Report: Fiscal Year 1962* (Washington, D.C.: USGPO, 1963), pp. 366, 378.

Forces amounted to approximately $3 billion, as shown in Table 1. This amount is slightly more than 10 per cent of the total annual expenditure for elementary, secondary, and higher education in the United States.[3]

TABLE 2

ENLISTED GRADES: U.S. ARMED FORCES

Pay grade	Army	Navy	Air Force	Marine Corps	Coast Guard
E-9	Sergeant Major	Master Chief Petty Officer	Chief Master Sergeant	Sergeant Major Master Gunnery Sergeant	Master Chief Petty Officer
E-8	Master Sergeant First Sergeant	Senior Chief Petty Officer	Senior Master Sergeant	First Sergeant Master Sergeant	Senior Chief Petty Officer
E-7	Sergeant First Class Platoon Sergeant	Chief Petty Officer	Master Sergeant	Gunnery Sergeant	Chief Petty Officer
E-6	Staff Sergeant	Petty Officer, First Class	Technical Sergeant	Staff Sergeant	Petty Officer, First Class
E-5	Sergeant	Petty Officer, Second Class	Staff Sergeant	Sergeant	Petty Officer, Second Class
E-4	Corporal	Petty Officer, Third Class	Airman, First Class	Corporal	Petty Officer, Third Class
E-3	Private, First Class	Seaman	Airman, Second Class	Lance Corporal	Seaman
E-2	Private	Seaman Apprentice	Airman, Third Class	Private First Class	Seaman Apprentice
E-1	Recruit	Seaman Recruit	Airman Basic	Private	Seaman Recruit

Of the 2.7 million active-duty military personnel in the Armed Forces, about 87 per cent are enlisted. (The term *enlisted* is used to designate a person in the Armed Forces who does not hold his rank either by a commission or warrant.) The nine enlisted pay grades or ranks are shown in Table 2, with the noncommissioned officers (NCO's) comprising the six top grades of the enlisted ranks.

To fulfill the country's military commitments and to maintain the

---

[3] *Digest of Educational Statistics,* U.S. Office of Education Bulletin OE-10024 (Washington, D.C.: USGPO, December 1962), p. 20.

military establishment at its authorized strength, the Armed Forces
must procure and train over 355,000 new enlisted individuals annually, in addition to some 35,000 junior officers. (An officer is one

TABLE 3

OFFICER GRADES: U.S. ARMED FORCES

Pay Grade	Army	Navy	Air Force	Marine Corps	Coast Guard
	General of the Army	Fleet Admiral	General of the Air Force	(no equivalent)	(no equivalent)
O-10	General	Admiral	General	General	Admiral
O-9	Lieutenant General	Vice Admiral	Lieutenant General	Lieutenant General	Vice Admiral
O-8	Major General	Rear Admiral Upper Half	Major General	Major General	Rear Admiral Upper Half
O-7	Brigadier General	Rear Admiral Lower Half	Brigadier General	Brigadier General	Rear Admiral Lower Half
O-6	Colonel	Captain	Colonel	Colonel	Captain
O-5	Lieutenant Colonel	Commander	Lieutenant Colonel	Lieutenant Colonel	Commander
O-4	Major	Lieutenant Commander	Major	Major	Lieutenant Commander
O-3	Captain	Lieutenant	Captain	Captain	Lieutenant
O-2	First Lieutenant	Lieutenant (junior grade)	First, Lieutenant	First Lieutenant	Lieutenant (junior grade)
O-1	Second Lieutenant	Ensign	Second Lieutenant	Second Lieutenant	Ensign
W-4	Chief Warrant Officer (CWO), W-4	CWO, W-4	CWO, W-4	CWO, W-4	CWO, W-4
W-3	CWO, W-3	CWO, W-3	CWO, W-3	CWO, W-3	CWO, W-3
W-2	CWO, W-2	CWO, W-2	CWO, W-2	CWO, W-2	CWO, W-2
W-1	Warrant Officer (WO), W-1	WO, W-1	WO, W-1	WO, W-1	WO, W-1
	Cadet	Midshipman	Academy or Aviation Cadet	(no equivalent)	Cadet

who holds his rank by virtue of a commission or warrant issued in the name of the President of the United States as Commander-in-Chief of the Armed Forces.) The officer corps includes four grades of warrant officers and ten grades or ranks of commissioned officers, as shown in Table 3.

The ranks *General of the Army, Fleet Admiral,* and *General of the Air Force* are outside the regular rank structure and are conferred through special congressional action. Officer candidates in the military academies are included in the officer ranks.

Of the total military force, some 30,000 (or 1.2 per cent) are women in uniform.

Approximately one million civilian employees work with the Armed Forces; they represent a relatively stable segment within the establishment, typically employed for skills they possess upon entry into the Civil Service. Under the provisions of The Government Employees Training Act of 1958, and supplemented by service administrative arrangements, there is an extensive training and educational program for these civil servants. A discussion of this program, however, is outside the scope of this volume. The education program for dependents of military personnel stationed outside the United States is discussed on page 103.

The training and educational programs of the Armed Forces should be of interest to students of education for at least these reasons:

1. All, or substantially all, male youth over eighteen years of age in the United States are affected by military service. The Armed Forces system of induction and training has implications for counselors of high school and college students.[4]

2. The Armed Forces represents a large—if not the largest—adult education effort in the country.

3. The Armed Forces provide vocational orientation and training for large numbers of mentally and physically qualified youth who are casualties of the secondary schools: the high school dropouts.

4. The utilization of Negroes in the services should present a challenge to the civilian school system.

---

[4] N. Hans, "Military Education," *The Yearbook of Education-1958* (New York: Harcourt, Brace & World, Inc., 1958), pp. 412–20.

Negro enlisted men enjoy relatively better opportunities in the Armed Forces than in the civilian economy in every clerical, technical, and skilled field for which the data permit comparison. . . . Negro enlisted men constitute 9 per cent of those who could be considered as craftsmen or foremen, while Negro civilians constitute only 5 per cent of these occupational categories in the general economy. With some exceptions, a similar pattern holds true for officers as a whole.[5]

5. Of the total number of personnel in the Armed Forces, over 300,000 are commissioned officers. Since 1900, the officer corps, as a group and together with the Armed Forces as a whole, has grown faster than the population and faster than most professions.[6] A system of professional military education for these officers reaches back well over a hundred years and, to some extent, parallels the rise of graduate education in the United States.

6. An increasing interest in federal participation in education is evident. A fundamental aspect of this participation, which has not been sufficiently documented or explored, is represented by education in the Armed Forces.

Viewed in almost any way, the Department of Defense and its component parts are more heavily involved in the educational process than any other department or agency of the government.[7]

7. The Armed Forces make a substantial regular contribution of trained personnel to industry and to society as a whole.

8. The military plays a significant role in national policy formulation.

9. The conduct of American servicemen at home and abroad is rooted in their military as well as civilian training. In proposing a Code of Conduct for the Armed Forces, an advisory committee to the Secretary of Defense stated:

The conscience and heart of all America are needed in the support of this code, and the best of training that can be provided in our homes, by our schools and churches, and by the Armed Forces will be required for all who undertake to live by this code. . . . Modern

---

[5] *Report of the United States Commission on Civil Rights* (Washington, D.C.: USGPO, 1963), p. 179.

[6] Morris Janowitz, *The Professional Soldier* (New York: The Free Press of Glencoe, Inc., 1960), p. 54.

[7] *The Federal Government and Education,* H. R. Document No. 159, presented by Mrs. Edith Green, Chairman of Special Subcommittee of the House Committee on Education and Labor (Washington, D.C.: USGPO, 1963), p. 144.

warfare has brought the challenge to the doorstep of every citizen, and so the code we propose may well be a code for all Americans if the problem of survival should ever come to our own Main Streets.[8]

In this discussion of education and training programs in the Armed Forces, the terms *education* and *training* are frequently used interchangeably. In their discussion, Professors Clark and Sloan decided, probably wisely, that the best approach to the problem of differentiating between education and training in the military was to ignore it.[9] In categorizing the various programs, however, it seems useful to describe certain types as being predominantly occupied with training and other types as being essentially educational in nature. For the purpose of this monograph, training programs are those which develop specific skills and are job-oriented, while education programs tend to be more complex and their learning outcomes more general in nature. Training programs are more likely to deal with large numbers of personnel and expensive equipment and facilities, while education programs are more often than not smaller in volume and do not require extensive facilities beyond classrooms and laboratories.

Within the military establishment, the distinction between training and educational functions are usually delineated by functional and organizational titles. Within the area of education there is evident a trend toward differentiation between professional military education, a function of the Staff Schools and War Colleges, and specialized education, which is provided by both graduate military technical institutions and by civilian colleges and universities, usually leading to a degree in the major field of study.

The materials and data used in this monograph come from unclassified sources—that is, sources to which access is not restricted for any reasons of military or national security. Throughout the discussion reference will be made to the literature in this field.[10] Al-

---

[8] *The Fighting Man's Code,* Department of Defense Pamphlet 8-1 (Washington, D.C.: USGPO, 1955), p. v.

[9] Clark and Sloan, *op. cit.,* p. vii.

[10] A subject index to some sixty-five English-language military and aeronautical periodicals not included in the more familiar commercial indexing services is contained in the *Air University Library Index to Military Periodicals* (Maxwell Air Force Base, Ala.: Air University Library, published quarterly, with an annual accumulation). Although this index, begun in 1949, serves primarily the educational and research needs of Air University, it is available to other libraries on an exchange basis.

though sources of information in the military establishment are not as readily available as might be desired, more material is steadily becoming available.[11] The student in this field must learn the locus, within the Armed Forces, of responsibility for education. Once this is done and the proper procedure for requesting information is mastered, the data needed for serious study and research will be forthcoming.

Implicit throughout this discussion is the hierarchical nature of the Armed Forces. The officer-enlisted man dichotomy—or military caste system—has a long and interesting history, but it is outside the scope of this study. In the description of the various educational activities that follow, it will become clear for which category of personnel a given program is designed. The relative place of the enlisted men in the Armed Forces has been described as follows:

> The enlisted men subordinate to the officer corps are part of the organizational bureaucracy, but not of the professional bureaucracy. The enlisted personnel have neither the intellectual skills nor the professional responsibility of the officer. They are specialists in the application of violence, not the management of violence. Their vocation is a trade, not a profession. This fundamental difference between the officer corps and the enlisted corps is reflected in the sharp line which is universally drawn between the two in all military forces of the world. . . . The difference between the officer and the enlisted vocations precludes any general progression from one to the other. Individual enlisted men do become officers, but this is the exception rather than the rule. The education and training necessary for officership are normally incompatible with prolonged service as an enlisted man.[12]

In the discussion concerning the various commissioning programs, it will be noted that a relatively small percentage of the officers on active duty served in the enlisted ranks before being commissioned.

The Armed Forces are composed of essentially two categories of personnel: individuals who have chosen to make military service their careers and who serve from twenty to thirty years, and those

---

11 As an innovation, in the 1962–63 edition of its *Education Directory* (Washington, D.C.: USGPO), the U.S. Office of Education added *Part 5:* "Federal Government," listing names of professional personnel in executive departments and agencies who spend the major portion of their time in educational activities.

12 Samuel P. Huntington, *The Soldier and the State* (Cambridge, Mass.: Belknap Press, 1957), pp. 17–18.

who enter through the Selective Service System and are satisfying their military obligation as defined by the Universal Military Training and Service Act of 1951 (as amended). Under existing legislation, the Armed Forces offer as many as fifty different programs through which the military obligation may be met[13] including:

1. Enlistment or volunteering for a total of six years, active duty or Reserve, with the option of choice of service;
2. Induction by way of the draft with little or no choice of service and an active-duty tour of two years plus a four-year Reserve obligation;
3. Enrollment in the Reserve Officer Training Corps (ROTC) or other officer-training programs at the college level, followed by a period of active duty;
4. Enrollment in one of the five service academies;
5. Enlistment in the Ready Reserve for six years, with six months of active duty;
6. Enlistment in the National Guard or Air National Guard before age eighteen and a half, with no active duty obligation except in emergencies, but with a requirement to participate in Reserve training until age twenty-eight;
7. Enlistment in the Reserve for six years, including two years of active duty.

The defense establishment is a huge, complex, and costly enterprise. In its bid for manpower it is in competition with industry and the other professions and vocations. Its educational task is directly affected by the extent to which it can attract and retain competent people.

Administrative Organization: The Locus of Responsibility[14]

Under the Constitution, the President of the United States is the Commander-in-Chief of the Armed Forces. Thus, the ultimate responsibility for education in the Armed Forces is his. This responsibility is delegated to an executive department of the government, created in 1949 and known as the Department of Defense (DOD).

---

13 Statement by Norman S. Paul, Assistant Secretary of Defense (Manpower), *Nation's Manpower Revolution:* Part 8, Hearings before the Senate Subcommittee of the Committee on Labor and Public Welfare, 88th Congress, 1st Session (1964), p. 2573.

14 *United States Government Organization Manual 1963–64* (Washington, D.C.: USGPO, June 1, 1963), pp. 121–202.

It is successor to the National Military Establishment created by the National Security Act of 1947. The head of the DOD is the Secretary of Defense.

The DOD was created to provide for the security of this country and was designed to integrate those government policies, procedures, departments, and agencies that are concerned with national security. Among the statutory agencies included within the DOD are the Joint Chiefs of Staff, the Department of the Army, the Department of the Navy (including Naval Aviation and the Marine Corps), and the Department of the Air Force. The U.S. Coast Guard is a military service and a branch of the Armed Forces of the United States. In time of war it operates as a service in the Navy; at other times it is under the direction of the Treasury Department.

It was the apparent intent of Congress to provide for the unified direction of the military services under the control of the Secretary of Defense but not to merge these services, nor to establish a single Chief of Staff or a General Staff over all the Armed Forces. Subsequent amendments to the Act of 1947, together with Presidential executive orders, have tended to strengthen the authority and control of the Secretary over the military departments and services. In Executive Order 10952, dated July 20, 1961, the Secretary was delegated the direction and control of federal civil defense.

Except during general war, the Armed Forces as a whole can be considered as one huge training and educational enterprise; however, within the larger framework of the DOD, each of the following classifications, categories, or levels has its own unique educational responsibility.

The Secretary of Defense.   Although this office is not a separate legal entity within the DOD, it is identified and defined for the purposes of this monograph as the center of authority including the Secretary and those individuals who can and do act for him and issue orders and directives in his name. Within the office, the training and educational function is delegated to the Assistant Secretary of Defense (Manpower). He, in turn, has an assistant: the Deputy Assistant Secretary of Defense (Education). The responsibilities of this office include formulation of educational plans, policies, and programs for the DOD. This office provides policy direction, review, and coordination of the Armed Forces Professional Education and Troop Education Programs of the military departments, including supervision and policy direction of the U.S. Armed Forces Institute (USAFI) in Madison, Wisconsin. It recommends actions including initiation, transfer, reassignment, abolition, and consolidation of training and education functions. It is responsible for promoting cooperation and understanding between the DOD and civilian educators, educational institutions, and related organizations. The Defense Advisory Committee on Education in the Armed Forces (DACE) operates through this office. This committee is composed of a maximum of twenty-four regular members (or their designated representatives):

1. Five military representatives (one appointed by each of the services: the Army, the Navy, the Air Force, the Marine Corps, and the Coast Guard;
2. Five members ex officio, including the Deputy Assistant Secretary of Defense (Education);
3. The President of the American Council on Education;
4. The Executive Secretary of the National Education Association;
5. The Chairman of the U.S. Civil Service Commission;
6. The U.S. Commissioner of Education;
7. Civilian educators (not to exceed fourteen in number) designated by the Assistant Secretary of Defense (Manpower), normally for a three-year term.

The Director of USAFI, and the Director of the Commission on Accreditation of Service Experiences of the American Council on Education are associate members of the Committee. The Committee advises the DOD on educational problems and programs related to military requirements, provides information on standards and policies governing civilian educational practices, and assists in assuring that educational services and materials made available to the Armed Forces are of high quality.[15] This committee is an example of the various civilian advisory educational boards and committees found throughout the military establishment.

The Joint Chiefs of Staff (JCS). The National Security Act of 1947 formalized the JCS, and subsequent amendments have added to its stature and authority as the principal military adviser to the President and the Secretary of Defense. The JCS is the military staff within the DOD and is composed of a chairman, the Chief of Staff of the Army, the Chief of Naval Operations, the Chief of Staff of

---

[15] Department of Defense Instruction No. 120.25, November 20, 1961.

the Air Force, and the Commandant of the Marine Corps (when matters of interest to the Marine Corps are being considered). One of the responsibilities of the JCS is to establish doctrine for unified operations, training, and policies for the coordination of the military education of members of the Armed Forces. Within the Personnel Directorate of the Joint Staff, the Education Branch has responsibility for reviewing and recommending policies for joint education and for developing and recommending joint plans for the determination and filling of educational and training requirements. It also has staff supervisory responsibility for the joint schools and colleges discussed in Chapter VI.

Unified and specified commands. The unified and specified commands are the fighting forces of the Department of Defense, its raison d'etre. These commands make up the top military operating command structure. All other elements—administration, education, logistics, and research and development—are designed to support these operating tactical and strategic commands. These commands are relatively recent phenomena in our military establishment and are creatures of the JCS.

A unified command is composed of components of two or more services. It has a broad continuing mission, under a single commander. A specified command is normally composed of forces from only one service. Both unified and specified commands are established and designated by the President.[16]

Some of these organizations are:

    Alaskan Command
    The Atlantic Command
    The U.S. Southern Command
    Naval Forces Eastern Atlantic and Mediterranean
    The Pacific Command
    The United Nations Command
    The U.S. European Command
    The Strategic Air Command
    The U.S. Strike Command
    The North American Air Defense Command

These commands are composed of officers and enlisted men assigned from the services. Each of these unified and specified commands has a responsibility for team, unit, or group training in the

---

[16] *Dictionary of United States Military Terms for Joint Usage,* The Joint Chiefs of Staff (Washington, D.C.: Government Printing Office, February 1, 1964).

specific military mission with which it is charged. The specialized
education of the individuals who make up these commands is the
responsibility of the service the individual represents. For example,
the U.S. Strike Command (STRICOM) is a unified command composed of both Army and Air Force personnel. Each year it conducts
several large-scale field exercises or maneuvers involving hundreds
of planes and thousands of soldiers and airmen. Planning the exercise, conducting it, and evaluating its results is STRICOM's responsibility. The training of the men who pilot and maintain the planes
is the responsibility of the Air Force; the training of the soldiers is
the responsibility of the Army.

Defense agencies. Like the unified commands, defense agencies
are relatively recent arrivals on the scene. They are illustrations of
the centralizing tendency within the DOD and the increasing authority of the Secretary of Defense over the military departments.[17]

These agencies, with the dates of their establishment, are:

> National Security Agency (NSA), 1952
> Defense Atomic Support Agency (DASA), 1959
> Defense Communications Agency (DCA), 1960
> Defense Intelligence Agency (DIA), 1961
> Defense Supply Agency (DSA), 1961

The heads of NSA and DSA report to the Secretary of Defense;
those of DASA, DCA, and DIA to the JCS. Each of these agencies
is manned by individuals assigned from and trained by the military
departments. Each is responsible for taking these specialists and
training them further as individuals or as groups in the functions
unique to the agency involved.

The military services

The Department of the Army. The Army, the oldest of the services, dates from the Department of War, created on August 7, 1789.
Policy concerning educational budgets, programs, and student load
is determined in Army headquarters in Washington, D.C. The U.S.
Continental Army Command at Fort Monroe, Virginia, is responsible for conducting all individual and unit education (other than that
provided by the U.S. Military Academy and the Army War College)
within the continental United States. The commanding generals of

---

[17] *Department of Defense Annual Report: Fiscal Year 1962, op. cit.,* pp. 26–30.

the Army components of unified commands are responsible for the instruction of the units assigned to them. These commands are the U.S. Army Air Defense Command and the U.S. European, Pacific, Southern, and Alaskan Commands.

The Superintendent of the Military Academy and the Commandant of the Army War College report to the Chief of Staff of the Army through the Assistant Chief of Staff for Force Development.

The Department of the Navy. The Department of the Navy was established in April 1798, before which the conduct of naval affairs had been the responsibility of the Secretary of the Department of War. Within the Department of the Navy, responsibility for training and education is more widely diversified than in any of the other services and is divided among some eight naval organizations:

1. The operational training of ship crews and the coordination of all amphibious instruction is the responsibility of the fleet commanders, who report directly to the Chief of Naval Operations.

2. All phases of aviation instruction, afloat and ashore (including Marine Corps aviation), are charged to the Deputy Chief of Naval Operations for Air.

3. The training of advanced base units is administered by the Deputy Chief of Naval Operations for Logistics.

4. The Commander of the Military Sea Transportation Service (MSTS) is responsible for the instruction of his ship crews and activities.

5. The training of all Naval Reserve personnel is the responsibility of the Commander, Naval Reserve Training Command.

6. The Chief of the Bureau of Medicine and Surgery administers all medical and dental education.

7. The Commandant of the Marine Corps is responsible for the instruction of his personnel.

8. The bulk of the responsibility for the individual training and education rests with the Bureau of Naval Personnel (BUPERS). It not only develops and administers policy but also performs many of the functions normally done in the field in the other services. For example, it develops, produces, and distributes curriculums, educational materials, training aids, and evaluation devices.

The Naval Academy, by custom, operates largely as an autonomous unit, reporting to the Chief of Naval Operations through the Bureau of Naval Personnel.

The U.S. Marine Corps. The Marine Corps dates from action by the Continental Congress in 1775. It is centrally responsible for providing fleet Marine forces of combined arms, together with supporting air components for service with the fleet, and for conducting such land operations as may be essential to the prosecution of a naval campaign. The Commandant of the Marine Corps is responsible to the Secretary of the Navy. The formulation of policy for the instruction of individuals and components of the Corps, except aviation, is the responsibility of one of the Assistant Chiefs of Staff, in Marine Corps headquarters, designated as G-3. Aviation instruction in the Corps is delegated to the Deputy Chief of Naval Operations for Air.

The U.S. Coast Guard.   Under the provisions of the act of January 28, 1915 (as amended), the Coast Guard became a military service and a branch of the Armed Forces of the United States. It operates as a service in the Treasury Department except in time of war (or whenever the President directs) at which time it operates as a service in the Navy. It represents, in its historical development from 1790, an amalgamation into one service of the activities of the old Revenue Cutter Service, the Lifesaving Service, the former Lighthouse Service, and the Bureau of Marine Inspection and Navigation. It is responsible for saving and protecting life and property, enforcing maritime law, providing navigational aids to maritime commerce and transoceanic air commerce, promoting the efficiency and safety of the American Merchant Marine, and keeping ready for military operations.

The head of the Coast Guard, the Commandant, is assisted by a headquarters staff. Within this staff the training and educational function is delegated to the Office of Personnel.

The Superintendent of the Coast Guard Academy reports directly to the Commandant of the Coast Guard.

The Department of the Air Force.   The Air Force is the youngest of the military services and became autonomous within the military establishment under the National Security Act of 1947. Within Air Force headquarters, responsibility for the formulation and execution of policy for the individual training and education of Air Force personnel is lodged in the Office of the Deputy Chief of Staff, Personnel.

Field responsibility for individual education is charged to four agencies:

1. The Air Training Command, which provides individual training for officers and airmen (including basic training, indoctrination for all Air

Force recruits, flying and technical instruction) and is also charged with the recruiting function.

2. The Air University, which is primarily concerned with the professional education of the officer corps.

3. The Continental Air Command, which is charged with the instruction of the Reserve forces.

4. The Superintendent of the Air Force Academy, who reports to the Chief of Staff through the Deputy Chief of Staff, Personnel.

Unit or crew training in areas of their own responsibility is discharged by four major commands located in the United States (the Air Defense Command, the Military Air Transport Service, the Tactical Air Command, and the Strategic Air Command) as well as four overseas commands (U.S. Air Forces in Europe, Pacific Air Forces, the Alaskan Air Command, and the Caribbean Air Command).

The Training and Educational Task

Implicit throughout the discussion of education in the Armed Forces are certain factors that underlie and complicate the process. Five of the factors will be identified and discussed briefly.

The nature of the military mission. Inherent in military operations is the necessity for the man-at-arms to be capable of discharging a variety of duties, regardless of his particular specialty. Although this need may be less urgent when he is stationed within his country in times of peace, he must be prepared and trained to perform under combat conditions in which his unit must be self-sufficient—under conditions of stress. This factor may impose mental and emotional, as well as physical, demands that have no counterpart in civilian life.

The range of conflict. The commitment of the United States to the defense of its allies and the worldwide deployment of its forces have already been noted. These responsibilities imply that U.S. forces must be prepared to conduct military operations across the entire spectrum of conflict. They must be trained, deployed, and ready for sustained military operations ranging from long-term global conflict (as in World War II) to counterinsurgency and antiguerrilla actions (as in Laos and South Vietnam since 1962) to the relatively quiet patrol and police actions that followed the Berlin and Cuban crises. These operations also include the discharging of U.S. responsibilities in South Korea, where the contact made with the enemy on July 5, 1950, has not yet been broken off, though active hostilities were halted by a cease-fire agreement in 1953.

The terms *general war, limited war,* and *Cold War* have been added to the American vocabulary and indicate the varieties of conflict for which the individual must be trained. The military man must be trained to be quickly ready for tasks he may never actually be called upon to perform, and he must maintain this degree of readiness over long periods. This frequently involves prolonged periods of separation from his family. He must practice his specialty, not only in the temperate climate of the United States, but also in the Arctic, the desert, or in the jungle. He must also be prepared to instruct individuals who have little facility in the English language in the use of complex weapons and equipment, and be an effective representative of his country in any foreign assignment. The implications of exploration in outer space as well as in the ocean depths are also beginning to have impact on military planning and education.

The complexity of weapon systems.[18] An additional factor affecting the educational task is the increasing complexity of the devices with which warfare is waged. The last quarter of the nineteenth century witnessed the beginnings of the vastly increased pace in the evolution of weapon systems, and a quickening of the traditional contest between offensive and defensive measures for waging war. The scientific and technological advances that were accelerated during and after World War II have revolutionized, not only weapons, but also the associated communications and logistic support systems. In 1963, 3.966 million separate items of supply were needed to operate and maintain these systems.[19] Advances in medicine, aviation, rocketry, communications, plastics, textiles, computers, energy conversion, and nutrition, as well as more recent discoveries in LASER[20] techniques have created whole new occupations and skills within the Armed Forces. These new skills require more instructional programs of increasing length and sophistication.

---

[18] A weapon system is a total entity made up of an instrument of combat—a unit of striking power—such as a bomber, a guided missile, or a submarine, together with all related equipment, supporting facilities, and services required to bring it upon its target or to the place where it carries out its functions. *The United States Air Force Dictionary* (Maxwell Air Force Base, Ala.: Air University Press, 1956).

[19] *Department of Defense Annual Report: Fiscal Year 1962, op. cit.,* p. 404.

[20] Light Amplification by Stimulated Emmission of Radiation.

The magnitude, complexity, and cost of these programs have become a matter of major concern to the services.

In testimony before congressional committees and in articles for their professional journals, senior service officers have been unanimous in identifying the need for trained people as their most serious problem. Weapon systems have become so complex that, in some instances, from five to seven years are required to introduce a new system into the active defense force. While these new weapons are being developed, it is necessary to train the men who will use and maintain them. Thus, part of the training problem is to be able to forecast—to foresee—what training will be necessary. A breakthrough in weapon technology means that certain other weapons will become obsolete. This rate of obsolescence calls for a degree of flexibility in training programs that military men have never faced before. Because of obsolescence, for example, many missile programs were cancelled during the period 1950–63—a move involving billions of dollars and an attendant rescheduling and revamping of the related operation and maintenance training programs.

> To meet the ever-changing demands for training requires long lead times and a very flexible combination of resources that include fixed training centers and bases, mobile training detachments and equipment, contractual arrangements with industry, educational institutions, and correspondence courses. As new weapons enter our inventory, new training programs are developed to support them in an endless evolution brought about by our research and development.[21]

Increasing mental and educational requirements. As warfare and its associated weapons and equipment become more sophisticated, there is a corresponding increase in the mental and educational prerequisites for individuals needed to operate and maintain the systems. The Armed Forces, as a matter of policy, urge young men to complete their formal education before enlisting. The minimum goal of the Armed Forces is high school graduation for all enlisted personnel, two years of college for warrant officers, and a bachelor's degree for commissioned officers. The latest data available for all military personnel on active duty indicate that, as of

---

[21] *Department of Defense Appropriations for 1964: Part 4,* Hearings before a Subcommittee of the House Committee on Appropriations, 88th Congress, 1st Session (1963), p. 794.

December 31, 1962, approximately 73 per cent of the enlisted men were high school graduates, 24 per cent of the warrant officers had completed two years of college, and 65 per cent of the commissioned officers were college graduates.[22] There are also deficits in the optimum mental requirements of the services. All men eligible for military service take the Armed Forces Qualification Test (AFQT). This instrument measures an individual's general ability to take military training within a reasonable length of time. Percentile scores on this test are converted into the five mental categories as shown in Table 4.

TABLE 4

MENTAL CATEGORIES AND CORRESPONDING PERCENTILE SCORES,
ARMED FORCES QUALIFICATION TEST

Mental Category	Percentile Score
I	93 – 100
II	65 – 92
III	31 – 64
IV	10 – 30
V	0 – 9

Source: Department of Defense Appropriations for 1964: Part 3, Hearings before a Subcommittee of the House Committee on Appropriations, 88th Congress, 1st Session, p. 29.

Group V individuals are not accepted for induction into the Armed Forces. Experience has indicated that personnel in Group IV usually could not qualify for specialist training, were discharged at a high rate, and, provided far more disciplinary cases than their number warranted.[23] Based on this experience, the Army now administers—in addition to the AFQT—an aptitude test battery to those classified in Group IV. Those who perform satisfactorily on the supplementary tests are accepted. Those unsuccessful are classified I-Y—"Qualified only in War or National Emergency." Approximately 30 per cent of inductees are now being drawn from Group IV. The services accept few volunteers who score below the thirty-first percentile.

The Navy estimates that "to support the increasingly high intel-

---

[22] Selected Manpower Statistics, Directorate of Statistical Services, Office of the Secretary of Defense (Washington, D.C.: USGPO, July 17, 1963), p. 25.4. The data concerning warrant officers are as of February 1960.

[23] Statement by Norman S. Paul, Nation's Manpower Revolution, op. cit., p. 2574.

lectual requirements for skill training and for advancement to the
petty officer ranks [it] would have to enlist mental groups in the
following percentages: 10.3 per cent in Group I, 49.4 per cent in
Group II, 32.4 per cent in Group III, and 7.9 per cent in Group
IV."[24] The requirements of the other services vary, but they are
reported to be substantially the same as those of the Navy; none is
able to recruit the required numbers in the desired categories.

Many of the individuals in Groups I and II are never available to
the recruiters or the draft; they are in college or in one of the various officer-commissioning programs.

The Assistant Secretary of Defense (Manpower) reported in
1963 that one of the most significant recent trends in recruitment
has been the increased proportion of enlistees entering under specific school-training or occupational-training options. Instead of a
general recruiting program, the services are increasingly attempting
to match the enlisted men they recruit, in terms of aptitude and
occupational interest, with service job requirements. For this purpose, increased use has been made, in pre-enlistment screening, of
the more refined aptitude test instruments, previously used only to
classify men once they had entered the Armed Forces. This trend
toward selection in relation to specific training aptitudes has pro-
gressed furthest in the Air Force. Since 1958, the Air Force has
selected all its enlisted personnel on the basis of separate aptitude
quotas for four broad occupational-training areas. In the Navy and
Army, enlistments under special occupational-training or assignment options have accounted for one half and one fourth, respectively, of new enlistments during the fiscal year 1963.[25]

The retention of skilled personnel.   Finally, and high in order
of importance as a factor bearing on the training task, is the problem that the rapid turnover rate of enlisted as well as commissioned
personnel poses for the Armed Forces at many levels of operations.
This problem has three aspects: the first stems from the fact that, in
the absence of a general war in which enlisted men serve for an
indefinite time or at the pleasure of the Congress, the length of
mandatory active duty may be as short as six months. By the time

---

24 Richard Parker and Ronald Tarbox, "Man and Machine," *United States Naval
Institute Proceedings*, 89, 4 (April 1963), 84. Reprinted from *Proceedings* by per-
mission; © 1963, by United States Naval Institute.
25 Statement by Norman S. Paul, *Nation's Manpower Revolution, op. cit.*, p. 2575.

the recruit has completed any one of the many skill-training programs, his mandatory tour of duty (usually three years) will have
expired before the service has received an appreciable return on its
investment in terms of time, effort, and cost of training. Many of
the skill-training programs are quite expensive. The Air Force estimates that it costs approximately $25,000 to train a skilled elec-
tronics technician, and if he leaves the service at the end of his first
tour of duty, many of the resources of that service are tied up in the
process of training replacements.

The second aspect of this problem of turnover rate stems from the
degree to which skills needed in the military services have direct or
closely related civil counterparts. Thus, as men from the Armed
Forces leave to go into industry, the Department of Defense, in a
very real sense, serves as a training establishment for industry as a
whole. Although this strengthens the national economy as a whole,
it represents a real problem for those responsible for maintaining
the skill structure of the Armed Forces. Turnover rates in civilian
industry are usually highest among unskilled and semiskilled occupations, and lowest in skilled, white-collar, and professional categories. Unfortunately, the situation in the military services has been
just the reverse: the occupational categories requiring the greatest
training investment and the highest mental aptitude are experiencing
the poorest re-enlistment rates.[26] For example, in 1961–62, the re-
enlistment rate for servicemen who had completed their first tour of
duty was 27.4 per cent, as contrasted with 88.8 per cent for career
enlisted personnel. During the same period, for every 100 electronics
specialists trained in the Armed Forces who had completed their
first enlistment, 76 chose to leave the service, presumably to take
employment in industry.[27] The Navy reported that in April, 1963,
it was short 30,000 petty officers in highly skilled technical fields.[28]

The third aspect of the turnover problem relates to the rigors of
military life as compared with life in more normal civilian occupations. The services, individually and collectively, have striven to
improve living conditions, to raise rates of pay, and to increase the
amenities of service life. Servicemen, particularly during long peri-

---

[26] *Ibid.*, p. 2573.

[27] *Department of Defense Annual Report: Fiscal Year 1962, op. cit.*, p. 382.

[28] *Department of Defense Appropriations for 1964*, Hearings before a Subcommittee of the Senate Committee on Appropriations, 88th Congress, 1st Session,
(1963), p. 368.

ods when they are not actively engaged in military operations, tend
to view a military career in an unfavorable light. For example, life
in the Navy involves sea duty, close living quarters, proximity to
the work situation, relatively low pay, separation from family, and
long hours of duty—these combine to produce low re-enlistment
rates. The other services have comparable problems.

About 20 per cent of all personnel in the Armed Forces are
either in formal training programs or occupy assignments in support
of these programs. It is estimated that, if retention rates were at
desirable levels, the national defense budget could be reduced $5
billion annually, and the requirement for manpower, equipment, and
training would decrease accordingly.[29]

Training and Educational Requirements

The process by which the Armed Forces forecast their educational
requirements is an essential part of military personnel planning and
fiscal budgeting, and represents an example of large-scale educational planning and administration. A detailed discussion of the
process of military planning and budgeting is beyond the scope of
this monograph, but some insight into the procedures involved is
desirable in order to appreciate the complexity and importance of
the undertaking.

The only justification for military services in a nonbelligerent society is that they protect that society from an immediate or an anticipated threat. The military planning cycle begins with a review of
the international situation. This review, which is an ongoing process,
is termed *the estimate of the situation* or *the intelligence estimate*.
In arriving at these estimates, the efforts of various federal agencies
(known collectively as *the intelligence community*) culminate in the
National Security Council. This Council advises the President on
the integration of domestic, foreign, and military policies relating to
national security.[30] Among the members of the Council are the
President, the Vice President, and the Secretary of Defense. The
Central Intelligence Agency is under the direction of the Council.[31]

---

[29] *Military Pay,* Hearings before a Subcommittee of the Senate Committee on
Armed Services, 85th Congress, 1st Session (1957), p. 17.

[30] *United States Government Organization Manual 1963–64, op. cit.,* p. 56.

[31] *Ibid.,* pp. 56–57.

The President, having been advised by the Council, includes in his annual budget message to the Congress a request for the funds needed to meet and counter the threat—that is, for the funds required to develop the appropriate military capability, or posture, for this country.[32] Subsequently, the Committee on Armed Services of the House of Representatives holds hearings on the matter. The Secretary of Defense and each of the military service chiefs (and their principal staff assistants) appear before this committee, and later before other committees of the House and Senate, to explain and to justify in detail the requests for funds. The relevance of intelligence estimates to military posture, and of military posture to national defense expenditures, may be inferred from the following statement made by the Secretary of Defense to the Committee on Armed Services:

> Obviously, the value of another billion dollars spent for defense also depends on changes in the world situation and the military effort undertaken by our antagonists. A large increase in the Soviet defense budget, for example, could substantially increase the value of an additional increment in our own defense budget. A further tightening of tensions or belligerent actions against the United States or its allies might well increase the relative value of additional military effort. Our Communist opponents have greatly increased the range of conflict to cover virtually every aspect of human activity. And we, together with our allies, must carefully allocate our defense effort to insure that we can meet the challenge on every front and at every level. An assessment of the present and prospective international situation and the military programs of our principal opponents is therefore highly pertinent to any discussion of the defense program and budget.[33]

The defense posture presented to the Congress by the Secretary of Defense is the end result of planning by each service developed in terms of its role and mission in the total defense effort. These plans are projected in detail for four years in advance of the date on which they are submitted, and in broader outline for ten years. By its very nature, the military establishment is attuned to crisis, and insofar as possible these crises are anticipated. But an unforeseen

---

[32] *Posture*, used in this sense, denotes the military position or attitude from which the nation can act or react immediately. *The United States Air Force Dictionary, op. cit.*

[33] Statement of the Secretary of Defense before the Committee on Armed Services, House of Representatives, 88th Congress, 1st Session (1963), p. 288.

enemy threat, a change in public opinion, the wavering of an important ally, or a technological breakthrough at home or abroad can—and does—alter the nature of the threat and consequently necessitates re-evaluation and replanning. These factors and others have had an impact on all kinds and numbers of weapon systems and support efforts needed by the Armed Forces. They have also had a direct effect on the categories and numbers of personnel with appropriate skills needed to develop, deploy, support, and employ these weapons.

Training and Education Program Categories

The training and educational programs of the Armed Forces can be discussed and classified in a variety of ways and from many points of view—by service, off-duty and on-duty, resident and nonresident —but for the purposes of this discussion, and in order to indicate their extent and variety, these programs will be treated under the following headings:

Training and education of enlisted personnel. This section will include a discussion of the relatively brief but important period known as *basic training,* as well as the various programs leading to technical proficiency in the many skills necessary to operate the Armed Forces. It will conclude with a description of the educational programs designed to produce that essential element in any military force: the noncommissioned officer.

Officer training and specialized education. Commissioning programs for cadets and other aspiring officer candidates correspond in function to the period of basic training for enlisted men. The variety and content of commissioning schemes will be reviewed. At the lower commissioned grades, some of the skill-instruction programs are closely allied to those for enlisted men; nevertheless, they are treated separately because of the nature of the specialties involved. With few exceptions, the programs for prospective officers are more complex and extensive and require a higher level of intelligence and education as a precondition for successful performance. Many of the programs are professional in nature and are carried on in civilian colleges and universities.

Other courses of instruction, here termed *collateral,* are designed to instruct individuals or groups in skills and knowledges that are not necessarily related to any one military specialty but are considered vital to the practice of the skills under specialized conditions.

Professional military education. This category deals with education for the profession of arms, for officership, regardless of specialty. The discussion will include the schools and colleges operated by the separate services, and will conclude with a description of professional military institutions in which all the services participate at the national and international levels.

Unit training. Most of these categories are descriptive of instructional programs designed for the individual. In unit-training programs the emphasis shifts to groups of individuals and their behavior as groups and as units of the group. The range of instruction is quite wide, as is that of the size of the group, which may be a rifle squad, a missile-launch squadron, a nuclear-powered submarine crew, a task force involved in an amphibious landing, or the thousands of individuals involved in an air defense exercise.

Off-duty education. The Armed Forces provide educational opportunities for active-duty military personnel to continue their formal academic education regardless of their current educational level or physical location. These programs are provided to assist the individual to perform his service job more efficiently, to prepare himself for more responsible service jobs, and to increase his chances for promotion. They also maintain continuity in the academic or vocational training which the individual began before entering the service, and increase his value to the civilian manpower tool when he is separated from the Armed Forces.[34]

A discussion of the education of dependents of military personnel stationed overseas and in certain military institutions in the United States will also be included here.

This introductory chapter has given some indication of the size and importance of the educational task in the Armed Forces of this country. It has also identified the various levels of responsibility within the Department of Defense, indicated the manner in which educational requirements are determined, and divided the task into categories. In Chapter II attention will be given to the service programs designed to convert the young civilian to military life and to train him as a military specialist.

[34] "Federal Funds for Education," *U.S. Office of Education Bulletin,* OE-10009, No. 14 (1961), 140.

CHAPTER II

The Training and Education
of Enlisted Personnel

Those who expect to reap the blessings of freedom must, like men,
undergo the fatigue of supporting it.

Thomas Paine, *The Crisis* (1775)

Introduction

In the Armed Forces the process of training and educating the
individual enlisted man usually includes three phases: introduction
into military life, or basic training; training in a specific military
specialty; and finally (if he exhibits the potential) selection, training, and education for responsibility as leader and supervisor, with
the rank of petty or noncommissioned officer.

Basic Training

Basic or recruit training is the process of developing the physical
stamina, minimal knowledge, skills, and attitudes needed in an effective serviceman. It is the period of initiation into the service life.
By law, the Armed Forces must train the recruit for a minimum of
four months before he can be assigned to overseas military duty.[1]

Approximately 0.5 million young Americans enter the Armed
Forces for the first time each year. To the individuals, their parents,
and the counseling and guidance personnel in the schools, this military obligation represents a major point of decision. In an effort to
provide accurate and up-to-date information to prospective servicemen, and particularly to school authorities, the Department of Defense publishes each month of the school year *The High School
News Service Report*. This publication is distributed free of charge

---

[1] "No member of the armed forces may be assigned to active duty on land outside the United States and its territories and possessions, until he has had four
months of basic training or its equivalent." Title 10, Section 671, *United States
Code.*

to schools requesting it.[2] In addition, each of the services periodically publishes an occupational bulletin describing, in some detail, its training programs and opportunities. The North Central Association of Colleges and Secondary Schools has published an excellent bulletin describing the various ways in which the military obligation may be fulfilled as well as the training and educational opportunities offered by each of the services. Depending upon the availability of personnel and the attitude of school officials, representatives of the recruiting offices of the services visit schools and confer with counselors and students.

The Armed Forces Examining Station (AFES) is the point of entry for the recruit. In a period of one or two days he is given a physical examination, the Armed Forces Qualifying Test (AFQT), and a battery of classification tests developed by the service of his choice or the one to which he has been assigned. The AFQT score is used to determine his fitness for entry into the Armed Forces. The classification test results are used later during basic training when the recruit is interviewed by an experienced counselor (usually a noncommissioned officer). The results of tests and interviews, together with the needs of the services, are considered in placing the individual in a military specialty and in any training program required for it. If the recruit already has a usable skill, he may be assigned to a specialty immediately after basic training.

The recruit is sent from the examining station to a military installation and is assigned to a group of from fifty to seventy-five contemporaries under the instruction and supervision of noncommissioned officers. These instructors have varied backgrounds in specialized skills and occupations. The prime requisite for instructors is competence, experience, and motivation for service. The two categories of instructors are: (1) drill or tactical experts, who

2 *High School News Service Report* (Great Lakes, Ill.: Building 3109); *Army Occupations and You* (Washington, D.C.: Office of The Adjutant General, Department of the Army, September 1962); *United States Naval Occupational Handbook* (Washington, D.C.: Bureau of Naval Personnel, Department of the Navy, 1962); *Air Force Occupational Handbook* (Washington, D.C.: Headquarters, U.S. Air Force, 1960–61); *Your Life Plans and the Armed Forces,* 2nd ed. (Washington, D.C.: National Association of Secondary School Principals, 1958), prepared under the direction of the Defense Committee of the North Central Association of Colleges and Secondary Schools; and *For You An Officer's Career in the United States Armed Forces* (Washington, D.C.: The Department of Defense Advisory Committee on Women in the Services, n.d.), which outlines career fields and other opportunities open to women.

spend most of their time with the recruits in the field, and (2) subject-matter specialists, who typically lecture in classrooms. Instructors normally volunteer for this duty and are carefully screened before being assigned. Each service conducts instructor-training programs which these noncommissioned officers must complete satisfactorily.

The groups to which the new recruits are assigned are called *companies* in the Army, Navy, Marine Corps, and Coast Guard, and *flights* in the Air Force. Basic training typically lasts eight weeks. It may, however, vary from eight weeks in the Air Force to sixteen weeks in the Marine Corps. The Air Force gives a portion of basic training concurrently with technical schooling. The difference in time devoted to basic training by the several services depends upon the roles and missions of the services to which the recruit is assigned, and other subsequent training programs in which the trainee will participate. Basic instruction takes place at some fifteen centers throughout the country.[3] Most of these centers are located so as to minimize travel costs and to take advantage of climate favorable to outdoor training the year around.

Physical fitness is stressed by all the services (in varying degrees) during basic training, and instruction is given in the regulations and history of the service, military courtesy, rules of conduct, the Uniform Code of Military Justice, personal hygiene, emergency first aid, food sanitation and handling, and the recognition of military insignia. In addition to these common subjects, each service stresses aspects of training considered important for all recruits regardless of later specializations. Thus, the Army and the Marine Corps stress physical conditioning, rifle practice, and minor tactics; in the Navy, the Coast Guard, or the Air Force, on the other hand, basic training is more nearly an orientation for later technical training than for combat training.

Army. Basic training in the Army is designed to assure physically conditioning indoctrination, and drill in the fundamentals of soldiery. Emphasis is placed on teaching the soldier to fight effectively and to survive on the battlefield, preparing him for advanced

---

[3] "Basic Aspects of Service Life," *High School News Service Report, op. cit.,* pp. 16–18. Information for women interested in serving in the Armed Forces is contained on pp. 15–16, 35–60.

training, and instilling confidence in himself, his equipment, his contemporaries, and his superiors.[4]

The initial period, called *basic combat training,* includes 370 hours of instruction over a period of eight weeks. The number of men involved is greater in the Army than in the other services, because the Army relies on the draft, with the result that its replacement rate is high. In the period July 1, 1963–June 30, 1964, approximately 360,000 recruits completed basic training at nine Army training centers.[5] Of this number about 100,000 were members of the Army National Guard or the Army Reserve and served on active duty only six months. The Army's training task is further complicated because educational backgrounds among its inductees are more varied than those among the recruits of the other services.

Every recruit is taught to be a combat soldier, regardless of the branch of the Army to which he may later be assigned.[6] The training task involves taking a largely undisciplined youth from civilian life, conditioning him to military discipline, teaching him to protect himself in battle and to perform his duties even though tired, angry, or frightened, and motivating him to stay in the Army after his first tour of duty.

The instruction includes periods devoted to field bivouacs, mock battle exercises, practice in camouflage and concealment, construction of hastily built fortifications, hand-to-hand combat techniques, rifle practice (with silhouette targets that appear and disappear rapidly), practice infiltration courses (complete with barbed-wire obstacles and live machinegun fire overhead), and the penetration of

---

[4] "Male Military Personnel Without Prior Service," *Army Training Program (ATP) 21-114,* pp. 1–2. "Military Training," *Army Field Manual 21-5,* pp. 10–12.

[5] Eight-week basic combat training is carried out at the following Army forts: Dix in New Jersey, Knox in Kentucky, Jackson in South Carolina, Gordon in Georgia, Polk in Louisiana, Leonard Wood in Missouri, and Ord in California. Modified courses are given for women at Fort McClellan in Alabama; for conscientious objectors, at Fort Sam Houston in Texas.

[6] "The branches of the Army are grouped into arms and services. The arms are those branches whose primary mission is combat and direct combat support. The services are those branches whose primary mission is combat service support, or administration to the Army as a whole. Certain branches have missions in both fields. The arms are Infantry, Corps of Engineers, Artillery, Armor, and Signal Corps. The services are Adjutant General's Corps, Corps of Engineers, Finance Corps, Quartermaster Corps, Army Medical Service, Chaplains, Judge Advocate General's Corps, Chemical Corps, Military Police Corps, Woman's Army Corps, Transportation Corps, and Army Intelligence and Security Branch." "Organization and Function, Department of the Army," *Army Regulation 10-5,* p. 19.

"enemy" fortifications with the support of live artillery and tank fire. A specified portion of the training is done at night and under other conditions of reduced visibility. Each aspect of the training program has well-defined objectives. Periodically, the recruit is tested against these objectives and may have to undergo periods of retraining.

Navy. Basic training in the Navy is a twelve-week program carried out in Recruit Training Commands in Great Lakes, Illinois, and San Diego, California. It is designed to provide a period of transition from civilian life to Navy life, to inculcate understanding and appreciation of the workings of democracy and of the Navy's place in democracy, to develop a desire for self-improvement and advancement, to promote high standards of conduct, and to provide sufficient knowledge and skills in seamanship, ordnance and gunnery, and other naval subjects so that the recruit may be of early usefulness aboard ship. The period is divided into three major areas:

1. Military training, including physical fitness, military drill, sentry training, individual and group responsibilities, and military reviews.
2. Training in such subjects as rank recognition and responsibilities, religious and moral guidance, citizenship responsibilities, Navy organization, safeguarding of classified matter, Navy careers, naval history, naval customs and courtesies, first aid, personal and oral hygiene, water safety and survival (including the ability to swim fifty yards and to stay afloat for five minutes), damage control aboard ship, shipboard orientation, ordnance and gunnery, and Navy automotive driver improvement.
3. Administrative subjects, including physical and dental examinations, and instruction and practical training in the work aboard ship. During basic training considerable emphasis is placed upon team competition in such sports as softball and boat races.[7]

Marine Corps. Basic training in the Marine Corps is longer and more rigorous than in the other services, and is carried out at Parris Island, South Carolina, and San Diego, California. It is composed of an eighty-day period of recruit training followed by a month of individual combat training. The duty day is from 5:00 A.M. to 9:00 P.M. Physical conditioning, hand-to-hand combat, and rifle marksmanship are stressed. Frequent tests measure the recruit's progress. After completing the initial training period, the recruit is assigned to a Marine Infantry Training Regiment. Here the emphasis is on amphibious operations and on the ability to function

---

[7] "Curriculum for Recruit Training," *NavPers 9235A*, p. viii.

as a part of a four-man rifle team. The recruit fires every type of modern infantry weapon, including demolition charges, flame-throwers, rockets, and hand grenades. He is schooled in naval gun-fire and the use of cargo nets, air support, helicopters, and various types of landing craft. He participates in cross-country combat and reconnaissance patrols during the day and at night, and in good weather and bad.[8]

Coast Guard.   Enlistees without prior military service undergo twelve weeks of basic training at the receiving center in Cape May, New Jersey, or in Alameda, California. (The normal training load for both centers is 1600 men.) The program is similar to that of the Navy except that greater emphasis is placed upon operating small boats, swimming, and lifesaving.

Air Force.   As is true of the Navy, Air Force basic training is more a period of indoctrination than of combat practice. This stems from the fact that the Air Force, at least for enlisted men, is largely a technical service. The basic eight-week period is conducted in two phases. In the first five-week phase, training is carried on at one central base and comprises 200 hours of instruction including (in addition to drill and physical conditioning) training in survival techniques and the defense of Air Force bases against atomic blast and radiation. At the end of this period, approximately 70 per cent of the airmen enter technical courses; the second phase of basic training, consisting of 120 hours of instruction, is given in conjunc-tion with these technical courses. For those airmen who are not assigned to technical instruction, the second phase of basic training consists of three weeks of instruction at Lackland Air Force Base, Texas. These airmen are then assigned to duty in a less technical specialty, such as motor vehicle operation or roads and grounds maintenance, where realistic training can be given within the work environment.[9]

The Department of Defense estimates that in the fiscal year 1963 the cost of basic training for some 350,000 newly enlisted personnel was $712 million.[10]

Although the time devoted to basic training in the Armed Forces

---

[8] "Male Recruit Training Syllabus and Individual Combat Training Syllabus." Letters from the Office of the Commandant of the Marine Corps, March 1 and May 2, 1961, respectively.

[9] "Airman Basic Military Training," *Air Force Regulation 50-42.*

[10] See Table 1, Chapter I.

is relatively short, it is an important part of the life of the serviceman and is so regarded by the services for at least the following reasons:

1. During this period the recruit receives the initial impressions of service life that may be critical in his decision to make a career of military service or to leave it at the first opportunity.

2. During this period the groundwork is laid for later instruction in the specialty in which the recruit will serve.

3. This is the period during which the services can determine the area in which an individual will be most useful.

4. In this period, the recruit gets, for the first time, up-to-date information and real insight into military life—including pay, promotion opportunities, career possibilities, various service benefits—and a rigorous physical and psychological assessment which gives him some conception of how he compares with his contemporaries.

5. During this period, many a recruit finds that, for the first time in his experience, he is regarded and treated as an adult, and he is subjected to social and racial relationships that are totally new.[11]

Having completed his basic training, the serviceman is now ready for the next step in his career: preparation for service in his specialty.

Skill Training

The profession of arms is unique in several ways, but its singularity is probably most pronounced in the frequency with which its members are rated, examined, and tested. From recruitment to retirement, overt evaluation in one form or another is an ever-present fact of life for the serviceman. At regular intervals throughout his military career, the serviceman is evaluated by performance ratings. His success—measured in terms of promotion in rank—is tied to these evaluations. By the time the recruit has completed basic training, including a series of physical examinations, he will have been evaluated by batteries of tests designed to gauge his mental and emotional status, his aptitudes and interests, and (if he has had work experience) the level of skill he has attained.[12] The results of

---

[11] M. D. R. Foot, *Men in Uniform* (London: Weidenfeld and Nicholson, 1961), p. 161. This monograph is an excellent analysis of the various systems used by modern industrial societies to man their armed forces.

[12] The testing programs and procedures in each of the services are extensive and comprehensive. Discussion of them is beyond the scope of this monograph. Basic references are: "Enlisted Evaluation System," *Army Regulation 611-205;* "Advancement in Rating of Enlisted Personnel on Active Duty," *DuPers Instruction P1430.7D;* "General Military Subjects Testing (GMST) Program," *Marine Corps Order 1418.12A;* "Air Force Testing Manual," *Air Force Manual 35-8.*

these tests and the information gained in subsequent interviews are compared with the current needs of the service in assigning the recruit to training in a specialty. This procedure is the classification process.

Enlisted skill structure. Since the Civil War, the relative percentage of purely military or combat occupational specialties in the services has decreased markedly and civilian-type occupations—both for enlisted and officer specialties—has increased correspondingly at a rapid rate.[13]

The presence of over a million civilians, as well as 32,000 women, in uniform is further evidence of this trend toward the "civilianization" of specializations within the services. Another indication of this trend is the extent to which many functions in the services, usually performed by men in uniform, are now being contracted to firms employing civilians. Although there is no uniform pattern for the assignment of these contracts, in some cases civilian contractors are now providing janitorial and food services, refueling and maintaining military aircraft, operating primary flying schools, providing logistical air support to and among military installations, and transporting servicemen and their dependents overseas. To the extent that they are assigned these functions, the Armed Forces are relieved of the training task for these services in situations short of military conflict. In combat zones, such services—regardless of their civilian character—must be performed by uniformed personnel; with minor exceptions, only such personnel are subject to military law and discipline as defined in the Uniform Code of Military Justice and the Articles of the Geneva Convention concerning the treatment of prisoners of war.[14] An additional factor (particularly applicable to the Navy) that limits the degree to which civilian contractors are used is the necessity of providing jobs ashore to which seamen can rotate after a tour with the fleet.

The occupational specialties in the enlisted corps that are unique to the profession of arms are of three general orders: (1) those concerned directly with defensive and offensive close-quarter combat; (2) those necessary to bring firepower to bear on the enemy, but—in varying degrees—more remote from the enemy or target;

---

13 Morris Janowitz, *The Professional Soldier* (New York: The Free Press of Glencoe, Inc., 1960), p. 64.
14 Title 10, *United States Code.*

and (3) those required to maintain and operate systems and services that support the specialists in the first two categories.

Specialists in the first class are found principally in the infantry skills in the Army and the Marine Corps where, in spite of modern weapon technology, sustained close-quarter combat remains the basic skill. In the second class are found skills associated with some of the heavier weapons in the infantry, in tank crews, in the artillery, in missile-launch crews, on certain of the smaller attack boats and ships, in submarines, and in manned fighter and bomber aircraft. In the third order are the far more numerous skills associated with such specialty groups as administration, medical, legal, chaplain, logistics, armament, communications, electronics, transportation, and supply. Although every enlisted man, regardless of specialty, must demonstrate and maintain minimum competence in firing the basic weapon of his service, most of the skills are in support of the less numerous combat specialists.

A codification and description of the occupations and specialties held by enlisted personnel are contained in classification manuals that are part of the personnel management system of each service.[15] Collectively, these manuals list some 248 major occupational categories and over a thousand individual skills and specialties for enlisted men. Many specialties are common to more than one service or are found in all services. Examples are those in food services, administrative and clerical areas, automotive mechanics, and photography. Enlisted specialties range in complexity from those of light-vehicle driver, cook, or military policeman, to the technical skills required of a ballistic checkout equipment specialist, a meteorologist, or a senior electronics specialist.

Each occupational specialty is described in some detail in the service classification manuals. These descriptions usually include the code number, the appropriate military rank or range of ranks, the duties in detail, physical requirements, and prerequisite skills and knowledge (including mental, educational, training or experience prerequisites). Related civilian occupations are also given both in terms of those listed in the *Dictionary of Occupational Titles,* pre-

---

[15] "Manual of Enlisted Occupational Specialties," *Army Regulation 611-201;* "Manual of Navy Enlisted Classifications," *NavPers 15105C;* "Marine Corps MOS Manual," *NavMc 1008-PD;* "U.S. Coast Guard Enlisted Qualifications Manual," *United States Coast Guard Publication 311;* "Airman Classification Manual," *Air Force Manual 35-8.*

pared by the U.S. Employment Service and those listed in federal civil service manuals. Military classification experts and counselors use these related civilian job classifications to compare any civilian job experience of the recruit to a related military specialty or to advise the military specialists on how his skill may relate to civilian employment if or when he leaves the service.

A description of the skill structure of the five services is difficult because there is no common organization or terminology among the services. Over the years, each service has developed its own structure and nomenclature. Although this serves the purposes of the individual services admirably, it complicates interservice comparisons. In order to cope with this difficulty and to provide a uniform reporting device, the Department of Defense has developed an Enlisted Occupational Conversion Table. This table has resulted in a consolidation, for reporting purposes, of the services' 248 major occupational categories into nine occupational areas, further divided into 83 occupational groups, and with provision for much larger numbers of subgroups.[16] These converted occupational areas and groups are shown in Table 5.

TABLE 5

DEPARTMENT OF DEFENSE ENLISTED OCCUPATIONAL TABLE:
OCCUPATIONAL AREAS AND GROUPS

Infantry, Gun Crews and Allied Specialists	Infantry Armor and amphibious Combat engineering Artillery, gunnery, rockets Combat air crew
Electronic Equipment Repairmen	Radio-radar Fire control electronic systems (nonmissile) Missile guidance, control, and checkout Sonar equipment Nuclear weapons equipment Teletype and cryptographic equipment Automatic data-processing computers Other electronic equipment
Communications and Intelligence Specialists	Radio and radio code Sonar Radar and air, traffic control Signal intelligence/electronic warfare Military intelligence Combat operations control

[16] Department of Defense, *Occupational Conversion Table—Enlisted,* Group Code 121, (Washington, D.C.: Office of the Assistant Secretary of Defense [Manpower], October 1963).

TABLE 5 *(Cont'd)*

Medical and Dental Specialists	Medical care Technical medical services Related medical services Dental care
Other Technical and Allied Specialists	Photography Drafting, surveying, and mapping Weather Ordnance disposal and diving Scientific and engineering aides Musicians Technical specialists, NEC *
Administrative Specialists and Clerks	Personnel Administration Clerical personnel Data-processing Accounting, finance, and disbursing Supply and logistics Religious, morale, and welfare Information and education Communications center operations
Electrical/Mechanical Equipment Repairmen	Aircraft Automotive Wire communications Missile, mechanical, and electrical Armament and munitions Shipboard propulsion Power-generating equipment Precision equipment Aircraft launch equipment Other mechanical and electrical equipment
Craftsmen	Metalworking Construction Utilities Construction equipment operation Lithography Industrial gas and fuel production Fabric, leather, and rubber Firefighting and damage control Marine operating crafts Other craftsmen
Service and Supply Handlers	Food service Motor transport Materiel receipt, storage, and issue Military police Personal service Auxiliary labor Forward-area equipment support

Source: Department of Defense Group Code 121, Office of Assistant Secretary of Defense (Manpower).
* Not Easily Classified.

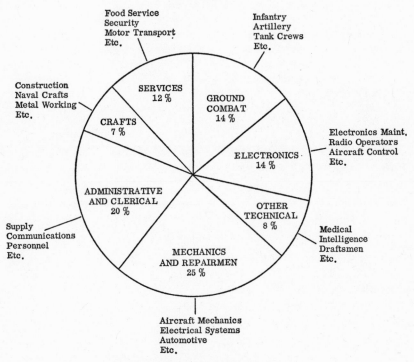

THE ENLISTED SKILL STRUCTURE, 30 JUNE 1963

Total Enlisted Jobs *
2,030,000

Food Service
Security
Motor Transport
Etc.

Infantry
Artillery
Tank Crews
Etc.

Construction
Naval Crafts
Metal Working
Etc.

SERVICES
12 %

GROUND
COMBAT
14 %

CRAFTS
7 %

Electronics Maint.
Radio Operators
Aircraft Control
Etc.

ELECTRONICS
14 %

ADMINISTRATIVE
AND CLERICAL
20 %

OTHER
TECHNICAL
8 %

Supply
Communications
Personnel
Etc.

Medical
Intelligence
Draftsmen
Etc.

MECHANICS
AND REPAIRMEN
25 %

Aircraft Mechanics
Electrical Systems
Automotive
Etc.

* Excludes about 320,000 trainees, transients and other
"bulk" positions without occupational designation.

Figure 1. *Source: Nation's Manpower Revolution:* Part 8, Hearings before Sub-committee on Employment and Manpower of the Senate Committee on Labor and Public Welfare, 88th Congress, 1st Session (1963), p. 2579.

The percentage distribution of enlisted personnel among the occupational areas listed in Table 5 was not available for the preparation of this monograph, but figures for a slightly different grouping of the occupational areas as of June 1963 are shown in Figure 1.

The technical complexity of the enlisted occupational structure is indicated by the fact that the categories of electronics, technical, mechanics, and crafts account for 54 per cent of the occupations.

> The most dramatic growth in occupational requirements [since World War II] has occurred in the electronics specialties. At the end of World War II, only six out of each 100 enlisted jobs was related to electronics equipment. By the early 1950's, this ratio had increased to about ten per 100. In 1963, it was 14.4 per 100, and—based on current projections—this growth is still continuing. For all services combined, our enlisted force now requires more electronic technicians than infantrymen; more aircraft mechanics than cooks and drivers.[17]

It is evident that relatively few enlisted personnel in the Armed Forces are assigned to purely combat specialties. The vast majority of enlisted men work in technical, administrative, and clerical areas, and at the higher skill levels—all of which require a considerable amount of formal training. In contrast, relatively few enlisted personnel are to be found in services and crafts for which the training requirements are relatively small. It is also obvious, as Wool has indicated, that the Armed Forces have very little need for the unskilled.[18]

Many of the tasks which could be accomplished by the unskilled have disappeared, largely as a result of developments in technology. For example, developments in electronics have largely eliminated the need for runners in infantry companies, and improvements in paint have greatly reduced the time spent in chipping paint and scraping rust in the Navy.[19]

---

[17] Statement by Norman S. Paul, Assistant Secretary of Defense (Manpower) *Nation's Manpower Revolution:* Part 8, Hearings before the Subcommittee on Employment and Manpower of the Senate Committee on Labor and Public Welfare, 88th Congress, 1st Session (1964), p. 2572.

[18] Harold Wool, "The Armed Services as a Training Institution," *The Nation's Children,* edited by Eli Ginsberg (New York: Columbia University Press, 1960), pp. 164–65.

[19] Kurt Lang, "Technology, Professionalism, and Careers in the Modern Military Establishment." Unpublished paper read at a conference of the Committee on National Security Policy Research of the Social Science Research Council, Princeton, N.J., June 20–21, 1963.

Instructional programs.   Whether the recruit will be sent to a school immediately after basic training depends on several considerations: his mental capacity for training, school vacancies in his specialty, his test scores, his civilian experience, and the need for men in his specialty at a given time.

If he is not sent to school, the recruit will go to an operating unit of his service, usually an on-the-job training assignment. Later, depending upon his interest and ability, he may be given a school assignment.

Relatively few occupations in the Armed Forces require no in-service schooling. Servicemen are taught to be postal clerks, cooks, and plumbers, as well as electronics and munitions specialists.

Each service has its own school system; however, enlisted men of one service are frequently sent to schools of other services as well as to civilian institutions and to training courses conducted by industries that manufacture new or prototype equipment for the services.

As noted in Chapter I, the enlisted grade structure is made up of nine pay grades, associated with military rank, from E-1 through E-9. The specialties in each major occupational group are related to these pay grades. There are five levels of competence:

Unskilled or entry-level	E-1, E-2
Apprentice or semiskilled	E-3
Journeyman or skilled	E-4, E-5
Advanced or supervisor	E-6, E-7
Superintendent	E-8, E-9

Each level of competence has its identifying numerical or letter prefix or suffix, used in association with the code number of the specialty. In order to progress from one level of competence to another, the enlisted man must demonstrate by performance or written test that he meets the service standards for that level.

An example taken from the Air Force illustrates this progression. One of the skill categories is Missile Maintenance, with an identifying numerical prefix of 44. An airman assigned to this skill could progress through the following levels:

44010	Missile Maintenance Helper	E-1
44130F*	Apprentice Missile Electrical Specialist	E-3
44150F	Missile Electrical Specialist	E-5
44170F	Missile Electrical Technician	E-6
44190	Missile Electrical Superintendent	E-7–9

* The letter suffix *F* denotes skills associated with the TITAN II Missile.

After basic training, the airman's record would show the Air Force Specialty Code (AFSC) 44010 while he was attending his first training school. Upon graduation he would progress to pay grade E-3 and his AFSC would change to 44130F. He would then be assigned to a missile squadron in the Strategic Air Command and would immediately begin preparing himself for examinations that would take him to the next higher AFSC and qualify him for advancement to the next higher pay grade. This is done by on-the-job training, by taking the appropriate Air Force correspondence course, or by taking courses given by a field training detachment. Depending upon his specialty, other periods of formal schooling might be required for progression in his skill and in pay grades.

The five services maintain approximately 300 specialized schools. The number and exact designations of these schools and courses change to meet service needs.[20]

Together, these schools offer more than 2000 separate courses of instruction, and in the fiscal year 1963 graduated over 370,000 students,[21] at a cost (as noted in Table 1) of just over $1 billion.

Courses vary in length from a few days to as long as forty-two weeks, but are typically one month long. Instruction is concentrated usually in one subject, and enlisted men are in the classroom or laboratory for a full day of six to eight hours. The instructors are skilled noncommissioned officers, petty officers, or civilians.

Comparisons between military and civilian training programs should be made with only a great deal of caution because of the great variation of courses and schools within each program. In general, however, the military training courses tend to be shorter, narrower in scope, less theoretical, and more directly related to military job needs.[22] This is true particularly for the entry-level training courses, where it is not considered economical to provide extensive

---

[20] "The Army School Catalog," *Army Pamphlet 20-21;* "Education and Training: Schedule of Classes Army Schools," *U.S. Continental Army Command Pamphlet No. 350-1;* "The Catalog of Naval Training Activities and Courses," *NavPers 91769;* "Official Bulletin of Schools and Courses: Fiscal Year 1964," *CNATT-P-5, Naval Air Technical Training Command:* "Catalog of (Naval) Hospital Corps Schools and Courses," *BuMedinst 1510.9A;* "Catalog of (Naval) Dental Technician Schools and Courses," *NavMed P-5029;* "Marine Corps Formal Schools Manual," *MCO P1500.12B;* "Coast Guard Enlisted Resident Training Schools," *United States Coast Guard Instruction 1859;* "The USAF Formal Schools Catalog," *Air Force Manual 50-5.*

[21] Statement by Norman S. Paul, *Nation's Manpower Revolution, op. cit.*
[22] *Ibid.*

and expensive training for the typical enlisted man, who will leave the service after he has completed his minimum military obligation. The formal training and the on-the-job experience of the career enlisted specialist often produce a level of qualification which compares quite favorably with that of the technician trained in civilian institutions.

The categories of skill training in the services may be generally described as entry-level, intermediate-level, and advanced-level.

Entry level. About 75 per cent of new recruits leave the service after their first enlistment. In order to maximize the productive time they will have while in service—and in contrast to the civilian work situation—the services have tended to fragment the more technical specialties into groups of skills that can be taught in a relatively short length of time in the entry-level courses. This practice permits the services to utilize the recruit at the apprentice or semiskilled levels.

Most of the servicemen found in these courses are serving their first enlistment and have just completed basic training. More experienced and senior enlisted men, however, will also be taking entry-level skill training either as refresher courses or because they have transferred to training in new skills that are needed to replace skills that are becoming obsolescent, that are in excess of service needs, or because the instruction is considered related or collateral to the specialty in which the enlisted man is currently working.

Intermediate-level. If the recruit re-enlists, or "goes regular," more expensive and, typically, longer courses are available. The opportunity for this higher level of instruction is considered important in influencing the first-termer's decision to re-enlist. Combined with additional on-the-job training and service correspondence courses, and predicated upon passing the appropriate tests, this period of intermediate training ·qualifies the enlisted man at the journeyman or skilled level.

Advanced-level. Until about 1960, the enlisted specialist was barred from the higher noncommissioned ranks on his specialty alone. The levels of E-6–9 were reserved almost exclusively for the noncommissioned officer or petty officer who functioned as a supervisor and who had attained his grade after many years of service and after having demonstrated his ability as a leader of men. More recently, however, the need for retaining these highly skilled technicians opened these highest levels of rank and salary. The more sophisticated, expensive, and lengthy types of specialized training are given at this level.

Nonresident Instructional Programs

The Armed Forces make wide use of correspondence courses in training programs. More than a million servicemen are pursuing military home-study courses. These courses are not to be confused with the civilian high school, vocational, and college correspondence courses offered to servicemen through the United States Armed Forces Institute (USAFI) at Madison, Wisconsin. Each service has at least one activity whose major responsibility is a program of correspondence study. These activities offer free courses in both skill and professional military subjects and are designed for individual or group study. They are usually based on instruction given by the residence service schools and are frequently written by the resident staff.

Correspondence study in the military differs from that in the civilian community because it is often done during duty hours and quite frequently is an integral part of the over-all training of the individual. Thus a highly skilled specialist may complete the various stages of his training through a combination of resident courses, on-the-job training, and correspondence study. Perhaps the most significant difference is the high participation rate—more than 30 per cent of military personnel—which must be considerably higher than the rate of the general population in the same age brackets. The high degree of motivation is responsible for this high rate, because these courses are directly related to promotions in rank. Furthermore, large numbers of military personnel stationed in remote places, such as radar and missile sites and aboard ships at sea, have a considerable amount of time to devote to these courses.

The services consider correspondence study, within its inherent limitations, an effective method of instruction, and probably no other type of program conducted by the military reaches so many people for so comparatively small an expenditure of funds.

The Army has twenty-one centers that prepare and administer correspondence courses, and the Navy has five such centers. All correspondence instruction in the Marine Corps, the Coast Guard, and the Air Force is administered by a single agency. The combined offerings of the services total more than 1700 courses.[23]

The Armed Forces
Information and Education Program

In addition to the more formal instruction given during basic training, skill training, and correspondence programs, the serviceman experiences a number of less formalized but important aspects of training and indoctrination throughout his career. These are known collectively as *The Armed Forces Information and Education Program*. This is sometimes referred to as *nonmilitary* or *why-we-fight* instruction.

This program includes instruction on the Code of Conduct, the place and role of each service in the defense establishment, American principles and ideology, current national goals and purposes, and international affairs. The program also provides information on the nature and purposes of Communism. It emphasizes to the serviceman the importance of his being an effective representative of his service in the civilian community, and of his country in the foreign community when he is on an overseas assignment.

Although the responsibility for the instruction and for the attainment of these goals resides in each service, the Department of Defense gives over-all guidance to this program and produces and distributes a wide range of instructional materials. Within the Department, this function is carried out by the Deputy Assistant Secretary (Education). These functions include:[24]

1. The development of policies for the radio and television stations operated by the services, and cooperation with national radio and television networks, the Federal Communications Commission, and the U.S. Information Agency.
2. The supervision of the operations of the Armed Forces Radio and Television Service in Los Angeles, California. This agency plans and programs information and educational materials for radio and television

---

23 "Announcement of Army Extension Courses," *Army Pamphlet 350-60;* "List of Training Manuals and Correspondence Courses," *NavPers 10061-R;* "Marine Corps Institute Handbook," *MC10(P)1550.1A; United States Coast Guard Institute Bulletin* (July 1, 1963); *Catalog of USAF Correspondence Courses* (January 1963).
24 *General Information on Activities of the Office of Deputy Assistant Secretary of Defense for Education,* unpublished bulletin (February 1, 1963), 10–11.

used by the Armed Forces overseas and in hospitals. This includes providing weekly some sixty hours of programming on records and tape to radio stations throughout the world, and fifty-five hours of film to television stations. Daily programs are broadcast to all overseas areas in which servicemen are stationed.

3. The supervision of the Armed Forces Press Service, which furnishes over 1400 service newspapers with news, features, and editorials.

4. The production of pamphlets, fact sheets, and area pocket guides for servicemen who are to be stationed overseas (including information on absentee voting procedures and information on such personal matters as medical care and retirement).

5. The production and distribution of films and discussion guides on three major themes: democracy, the heritage of freedom, and the threat of Communism.

The services have their own programs for the use of these materials. They have been closely reviewed by the Senate Special Preparedness Subcommittee and an advisory committee appointed by the Secretary of Defense.[25] The annual cost for the production and distribution of materials is over $9 million.[26]

Supervisory Education of Noncommissioned Officers

The senior noncommissioned officer is sometimes referred to as the backbone of the services. Advances in weapon technology have resulted in such increases in the rapidity and force of ground fire that massed formations in attack or defense are extremely hazardous. These developments have resulted in a dispersion of combat forces on the battlefield and have placed added emphasis on the importance of initiative and leadership and on the judgment of the junior officer or noncommissioned officer who commands a rifle squad of from four to eight men. For these reasons the Army and the Marine Corps place great emphasis on the selection and training of noncommissioned officers for duty in the tactics of small units.

The noncommissioned officer is the link between the commissioned officer who formulates and issues orders and directives and

---

25 *Military Cold War Education and Speech Review Policies: Parts 3, 4, 6,* Hearings before a Senate Special Preparedness Subcommittee, 87th Congress, 2nd Session (March-June, 1962); *Report to the Secretary of Defense of the Advisory Committee on Nonmilitary Instruction* (July 20, 1962).

26 *Department of Defense Appropriations for 1965: Part 2,* Hearings before a Subcommitte of the House Committee on Appropriations, 88th Congress, 2nd Session, pp. 616–17.

the enlisted men of lower ranks who execute these orders and directives. Traditionally, the noncommissioned officer was a mature professional with extensive service experience. He was a leader rather than a specialist. The men he supervised were younger and had less service.

The situation in the Armed Forces is markedly different now. Because of the expanding need for skilled technicians, many noncommissioned officers have attained their rank with little or no supervisory or leadership experience. In the Navy, the Coast Guard, and the Air Force, the role of the senior noncommissioned officer or petty officer is comparable to that of the foreman in industry—but with important differences. For example, one of the central responsibilities of the supervisor in industry is to deal with labor unions at the shop level. Although the noncommissioned officer usually does not have this problem, he may—unlike his civilian counterpart—be responsible for his subordinates around the clock and seven days a week. Their personal welfare and conduct is his concern; he is responsible for the discipline and morale of his unit.

To a greater degree than is true of the foreman in industry, the noncommissioned officer is an instructor. The services typically pick highly competent and experienced noncommissioned officers as instructors of recruits in basic training. The Marine Corps lays particular stress on the selection and training of its drill instructors, who bear the major responsibility for basic training. In the day-to-day operation of a small unit, the noncommissioned officer or petty officer is the pivotal figure in on-the-job training.

In the Air Force some responsibilities formerly discharged by junior commissioned officers are now being assigned to senior noncommissioned officers of grades E-7 and higher. These responsibilities involve the signing of certain types of documents, the handling of certain classes of funds, the custody of particular types of supplies, and the control of certain categories of top secret materials. In the Navy and the Coast Guard, senior petty officers may be captains of a particular class of small boats, usually Navy yard-craft-type vessels such as crash boats, floating cranes, and the like. In the Army and the Marine Corps the noncommissioned officer must be an expert in the tactical employment of small units, and he is expected to lead the unit in the absence of the officer in charge. Thus, to a degree, the noncommissioned officer in the Army and the Marine Corps is more of a leader, while in the Navy and the Air Force his central role is that of a supervisor. The training programs in the different services reflect these divergent roles.

Although there is no fixed point in the grade structure that separates the specialist from the supervisor, the technician—in order to progress to the more senior noncommissioned officer grades—must begin to take on some supervisory responsibilities at about the E-5 level. Before 1960 it would have been unusual for an enlisted man to progress beyond the E-7 level on his technical skill alone, but because of the alarming turnover rate among specialists, the services have revised promotion procedures: it is now possible for the specialist to attain the highest enlisted rank with little or no supervisory duties. Thus one of the major personnel problems faced by the services is the provision of a career incentive, other than military rank, for the highly skilled technical specialist. This situation is reflected in the distribution of grades in the enlisted corps. For example, in June 1962, of the total number of uniformed men and women in the Armed Forces, 86.9 per cent were in the enlisted corps. The grade distribution is shown in Table 6.

TABLE 6

ENLISTED PERSONNEL BY GRADE

Pay Grade	Number
E-9	7,310
E-8	25,077
E-7	121,453
E-6	222,075
E-5	376,983
E-4	426,956
E-3	545,231
E-2	315,794
E-1	117,651
Total	2,158,530

Source: Annual Report of the Secretary of Defense for Fiscal Year 1962 (Washington, D.C.: USGPO, 1963), p. 372.

The procedures for advancement in grade vary to some degree among the services, but they are substantially the same. The procedure used in the Navy is fairly typical: advancements in grade are acomplished through a Navywide system of competition in all petty-officer grades, E-4 and higher. Advancements are based on demonstrated proficiency in assigned duties, on the evaluation and recommendation of the commanding officer, and on the results of written examinations. All eligible personnel compete for advancement to fill vacancies throughout the Naval establishment. Examinations for all pay grades are developed by the Naval Examining Center, Great Lakes, Illinois.[27] These examinations are administered by examining boards located at the various stations and on ships where naval personnel are stationed. They are scored by the Naval Examining Center with modern, high-speed equipment. The test results are combined with other factors which affect the advancement of personnel from grades E-4–7. Selection for promotion for grades E-8 and E-9 is made by a board convened in the Navy Department.[28]

All the services have resident schools for training noncommissioned and petty officers in managerial, supervisory, and leadership responsibilities. The minimum length of these courses is four weeks. The schools are called *academies* in the Army, the Air Force, and the Marine Corps, and *leadership schools* in the Navy and the Coast Guard.[29] Entrance to these schools is based on proven capacity for greater responsibility. A typical curriculum outline would include the following subject headings:

> The Uniform Code of Military Justice
> Service History
> Leadership and Human Relations
> Supervision and Management
> Communication Skills
> Conference Leadership and Problem-solving
> Teaching Techniques
> Drills and Ceremonies
> Physical Conditioning and Training

In the Army and in the Marine Corps, the curriculum includes Minor Tactics, Map-reading, and Weapons.

The purpose of these training programs is to broaden the pro-

---

27 The comparable centers for test development in the other services are: The Army's Adjutant General's School, Indianapolis, Ind.; The Marine Corps Schools, Quantico, Va.; The Coast Guard Institute, Groton, Conn.; and The Air Force Personnel Laboratory, Lackland Air Force Base, Texas.

28 "Advancement in Rating of Enlisted Personnel on Active Duty," *op. cit.*

29 "Noncommissioned Officers Academies," *Army Regulation 350-90;* "Curriculum for U.S. Naval Schools, Leadership Class C-1," *NavPers 92608A;* "Noncommissioned Officer Training," *Air Force Regulation 50-39.*

fessional knowledge of the noncommissioned officer, to increase his self-confidence, and to give him the sense of responsibility required of a competent supervisor and a leader of men. His training does not stop with these formal courses, for under the guidance of the commissioned officers with whom he is associated he is a student of supervision as well as a teacher of his subordinates, and he is rated regularly on his ability as a supervisor.

The path to commissioned rank is open to the noncommissioned officer, and each service encourages its more promising noncommissioned officers to apply for training in the various officer-candidate programs.

CHAPTER III

Officer Training and Specialized Education

In the conditions of modern life the rule is absolute: the race which does not value trained intelligence is doomed. Not all your heroism, not all your social charm, not all your wit, not all your victories on land or at sea, can move back the finger of fate. Today we maintain ourselves. Tomorrow, science will have moved forward yet one more step, and there will be no appeal from the judgment which will then be pronounced on the uneducated.

Alfred North Whitehead, *The Aims of Education* (1947)

Introduction

The military establishment of the United States is made up of the active force and the Reserve force. The officer corps of the active force is composed of those with Regular commissions and those with Reserve commissions.[1] These Reserve officers can be further divided into those that are serving their obligatory tours of duty— usually three to five years—and those who have declared their intention to remain on extended active duty. The Reserve force, which includes the National Guard, is made up of three components: the Ready Reserve, the Standby Reserve, and the Retired Reserve. The Ready Reserves can be ordered to duty by the President alone; the other two categories of Reserves cannot be ordered to duty without the approval of Congress.

On June 30, 1962, 343,121 officers were on active duty with the Armed Forces of the United States.[2] As a group, these officers made up 12.2 per cent of the total active military force for that year. The size and composition of the officer corps is regulated by congressional authority. The active-duty corps consisted of 159,685 officers with Regular commissions and 183,436 with Reserve commissions.

---

[1] Regular commissions are made by the President with the advice and consent of the Senate. Reserve commissions are made by direction of the President and delegated to the services. Approximately 60 per cent of the officers of the active force are Regular officers; approximately 40 per cent are Reserve officers. Regular officers are selected from graduates of the service academies, of ROTC programs, and—to a lesser extent—of OCS.

[2] *Department of Defense Annual Report: Fiscal Year 1962* (Washington, D.C.: USGPO, 1963), p. 376. The total includes 3164 Coast Guard officers on active duty.

The term *career officers,* as used here, includes Reserve officers on extended active duty and officers with Regular commissions.

Commissioning Programs

To compensate for losses from death, retirement, voluntary separation at the end of obligatory tours, resignation, and other causes, the services commission approximately 35,000 officers annually. Some indication of the relative importance of various commissioning programs as sources of officer personnel is shown in Table 7,

TABLE 7

SOURCE OF COMMISSION OF ACTIVE-DUTY OFFICERS,
PERCENTAGE DISTRIBUTION

Source of Commission	Army	Navy	Marine Corps	Coast Guard	Air Force
Academies	8.3	14.39	2.5	48.0	3.72
ROTC	45.4	10.54	12.6		23.62
OCS		4.35	59.0	26.6	6.15
Enlisted programs	24.9	34.10	13.1	20.67	9.85
Direct commissions	15.8	12.66	.1	0.03	10.63
Aviation cadets		20.84	11.2		40.38
Other	5.6	3.02	1.5	4.70	5.65

Source: Army data is from a sample survey of 7757 officers, excluding female personnel and general officers, as of November 1962; Navy, January 1964; Air Force, May 1963. Data on Marine Corps is for officer accessions 1952–63, rather than on total officers on active duty.

showing the percentage distribution of officers on active duty by source of commission. From the data in this table it is evident that the service academies provide a relatively small percentage of the total number of officers in all the services, with the exception of the Coast Guard.[3] In the Army, 70 per cent of the officers on active duty received their commissions through the ROTC program (45 per cent) or programs for enlisted men (25 per cent). A large source for the Air Force and, to some extent, for the Navy and the Marine Corps has been the Aviation Cadet programs developed for the greatly expanded pilot-training programs of World War II. Table 7 also shows that each service has programs that enable en-

---

[3] This relatively high percentage of academy graduates in the Coast Guard is explained by the fact that there are only some 3000 officers in its active force, and the academy graduates about ninety officers annually.

listed personnel to become commissioned officers. The Navy, the Army, and the Coast Guard have obtained substantial proportions of their officers from the enlisted ranks.

In order to compete with one another and with the recruiting programs of the other professions, industry, and civilian life in general, the services currently have a wide variety of officer-procurement programs.

Federal academies. The five federal academies are listed here chronologically: U.S. Military Academy, West Point, New York (1802); U.S. Naval Academy, Annapolis, Maryland (1845); U.S. Coast Guard Academy, New London, Connecticut (1876); U.S. Merchant Marine Academy, King's Point, Long Island, New York (1942);[4] U.S. Air Force Academy, Colorado Springs, Colorado (1954). The Army, the Navy, and the Air Force maintain academy preparatory schools that were established primarily to provide intensive review instruction for enlisted personnel selected to enter the academies.

As shown in Table 8, the five federal academies enroll about

TABLE 8

ANNUAL ENROLLMENT, GRADUATES, OPERATING COST, COST PER STUDENT
AND COST PER GRADUATE FOR FEDERAL ACADEMIES,
FISCAL YEAR 1962

Service Academy	Enroll- ment	Gradu- ates *	Operating Cost	Annual Cost per Student	Cost per Gradu- ate **
Army	2,400	500	$27,741,000	$11,558	$45,650
Navy	3,742	797	28,870,000	7,768	30,980
Coast Guard	600	80	4,065,000	6,775	†
Merchant Marine	983	270	3,170,000	3,224	†
Air Force	2,267	298	28,071,000	12,382	47,120
	9,992	1,945	$91,917,000		

Source: The Federal Government and Education, H. R. Document No. 159, presented by Mrs. Edith Green, Chairman of Special Subcommittee of the House Committee on Education and Labor (Washington, D.C.: USGPO, 1963), p. 144.
* *American Universities and Colleges*, 8th ed. (Washington, D.C.: American Council on Education, 1960).
** *Reserve Officer Training Corps Program*, H. R. Report No. 925, 88th Congress, 1st Session (November 26, 1963), pp. 10–13.
† Information not available.

4 Although the United States Merchant Marine is not a military service, graduates of its academy, in addition to being commissioned in the Merchant Marine, may be commissioned ensigns in the Naval Reserve and the Coast Guard Reserve.

10,000 students, called *cadets* in the Army and the Air Force, and *midshipmen* in the Navy, the Coast Guard, and the Merchant Marine. In 1960–61 these academies produced nearly 2000 graduates at an annual operating cost of about $91 million and a cost per student ranging from $3224 to $12,382. In 1963 the reported total cost per graduate of these four-year courses ranged from $30,980 at the Naval Academy to $47,120 at the Air Force Academy.[5] (One possible reason for the difference in cost was the larger enrollment at Annapolis.) Legislation enacted by the 88th Congress will result in increasing the enrollment of the Army and the Air Force Academies to that of the Naval Academy between 1965 and 1968. This legislation will ultimately have the effect of producing some 2400 graduates annually from the academies. It is understood that the Coast Guard will increase its enrollment to produce approximately 100 graduates annually.

The academies are four-year undergraduate institutions; each is approved by the appropriate regional accrediting association. Graduates are awarded a Bachelor of Science degree and a commission in the Regular establishment of their service. The rank upon graduation is second lieutenant in the Army, the Air Force, and the Marine Corps, and ensign in the Navy, the Coast Guard, and the Merchant Marine.

The academies are inspected each year by statutory boards of visitors that prepare written reports to the President of the United States. The curriculums of the academies are divided between the more traditional undergraduate academic subjects and professional military subjects and exercises. Each academy emphasizes physical education, including intramural and intercollegiate athletic programs.

Traditionally, the curriculums of the academies were rather heavily oriented toward engineering and other technical subjects. Although this is still true to some extent, particularly in the Coast Guard and Merchant Marine Academies, since World War II the institutions have tended to offer a more balanced program of studies with additional offerings in the social sciences and the humanities.

---

[5] A word of caution concerning the interpretation of unit costs in the services is appropriate here. The above data are cited because they give some conception of order of magnitude, not because they are necessarily comparable. The factors used in determining such costs and others given throughout this volume are decided upon by each service; consequently, any variation may be more the result of the difference in methods of computation rather than real differences in cost.

Because many cadets and midshipmen enter the academies after having attended college for a year or two, the academies are now tending to give recognition to such individual differences by enrichment programs and academic majors.

The Air Force Academy, in cooperation with Purdue and Georgetown Universities, has developed a plan for qualified cadets to begin graduate work during the senior year. These cadets then go on to complete requirements for the master's degree at one of the cooperating institutions. Purdue offers a degree in Astronautics; Georgetown, in International Affairs. It is understood that the Academy hopes to expand this program to a possible maximum of eight cooperating universities.

The professional military emphasis in the academies permeates the entire program, including the more traditional academic studies. Throughout the four years, cadets and midshipmen follow a rigid daily schedule and must conform to strict discipline and rules of conduct. Military training, however, is recognized as a separate phase of the program and is under the direction of a commandant of cadets, just as the academic phase is administered by a dean or other authority. The professional military instruction at the academies serves as the standard for the other commissioning programs of each of the services; to the extent that the time and facilities permit, ROTC and OCS programs are a reflection of what is done at the academies.

The military program consists of two types of activities. The first, usually conducted outside the classroom, is made up of a wide variety of exercises, drills, and ceremonies. It serves the immediate purpose of making a rapid transition from civilian to military life. The extremely severe discipline to which cadets and midshipmen are subjected immediately upon their arrival and during their first year has been characterized as a deliberate test of the depth of their commitment to military life.[6] But beyond this purpose, military training at the academies has the larger aim of developing qualities of leadership, self-confidence, self-control, as well as obedience to constituted authority, a spirit of public service, the cultivation of certain social graces, and adherence to a code of honor. Cadets are organized into groups under the leadership of student officers. As the cadet moves from his first to his final year, he learns to follow orders as

---

[6] Morris Janowitz, *The Professional Soldier* (New York: The Free Press of Glencoe, Inc., 1960), pp. 128–29.

well as to assume positions of increasing responsibility and authority over his juniors. It is this aspect of the academy life—the development of professional commitment and *esprit de corps*—that resembles in purpose the schools of other professions such as teaching, medicine, and theology.

The other aspect of the professional military program is designed to prepare the cadet for duty as a junior officer. The subjects and skills taught in the professional military area will vary to some degree among the services, but those listed below are characteristic of all academies:

1. The provisions of the Uniform Code of Military Justice.
2. Military history and the principles of war, beginning with Sun Tzu, in the fifth century, BC, and extending through such theoreticians as Machiavelli, Clausewitz, and Jomini to the more modern and contemporary strategists.[7]
3. The national security organization and the place of each service in this organization.
4. Service history.
5. Service weapons, and skill in firing certain small arms.
6. The traditions, customs, and courtesies characteristic of military life.
7. Personal hygiene.
8. Instructor training, including speech, instructional methods, instructional aids, and practice teaching.
9. Tactics and strategy.
10. Service skill structure and career planning, including professional and specialized postgraduate educational opportunities.
11. Case studies in military management and leadership.
12. Human relations and psychology.
13. Flight indoctrination in light aircraft.

In addition, each of three summers between school years is occupied with field trips or cruises and visits to combat installations, research centers, and overseas tours, to familiarize cadets with the military environment in which they will live and work.

When the academies were founded, and for some decades thereafter, they provided terminal professional education and were the source of service doctrine on strategy and tactics.[8] The Academy at

---

[7] Edward Mead Earle (ed.), *Makers of Modern Strategy* (Princeton, N.J.: Princeton University Press, 1943), pp. 284–485.

[8] Thomas E. Shaughnessy, *Beginnings of National Professional Military Education in America: 1775–1825*, unpublished doctoral dissertation presented at The Johns Hopkins University, 1956.

West Point was the first engineering college in this country. The term *civil engineering* itself was coined to distinguish curriculums whose emphasis differed from that at West Point.[9] America's expansion to the West—manifested not only in military conquest but also in the construction of roads, bridges, railroads, and river and harbor facilities—was largely the work of West Point graduates. This kind of public works function is still being carried on by the Army's Corps of Engineers. Technical developments in weapon systems, the experiences resulting from the War of 1812 and the Spanish-American War, and professional military developments in Europe led to the establishment of additional postgraduate professional military schools. For this reason, the academies are no longer terminal institutions but simply the first important stage in the professional education of the career officer. They provide the knowledge that is prerequisite to later graduate study in specialized subjects.

Reserve Officer Training Corps (ROTC). Instruction in military subjects in civilian colleges was introduced in 1819 at Norwich University by Alden Partridge, a graduate and former Superintendent of the U.S. Military Academy.[10] Military subjects gradually spread to other civilian schools. Virginia Military Institute was established in 1839 and The Citadel (South Carolina) in 1842. In 1862 the Morrill Act gave impetus to military instruction in civilian colleges and universities. The ROTC program was formalized, substantially as it is known today, by the National Defense Act of 1916.

Originally designed as a source of Reserve officers, who would take periodic summer training but would be called to active duty only in the event of a national emergency, the ROTC program is now the largest single source of active-duty officers in the Armed Forces. Thus, to an increasing degree, the term *Reserve* is a misnomer.[11] For the fiscal year 1963 the cadet enrollment was 291,927 in 486 Army, Navy, and Air Force units located on 320 college and university campuses. The ROTC program produced 26,772 commissioned officers at a cost of $83.7 million, with 2847 officers,

---

[9] John W. Masland and L. I. Radway, *Soldiers and Scholars* (Princeton, N.J.: Princeton University Press, 1957), p. 78.

[10] *Reserve Officers Training Corps Program,* H. R. Report No. 925, 88th Congress, 1st Session (November 26, 1963), p. 5.

[11] Gene M. Lyons and John W. Masland, *Education and Military Leadership: A Study of the ROTC* (Princeton, N.J.: Princeton University Press, 1959), p. 241.

2654 enlisted personnel, and 357 civilians on full-time duty in support of the program.[12]

The major reason for the relatively low production rate of the program in terms of the number enrolled—26,772:291,927—is the fact that in many of the institutions, particularly the land-grant universities, participation by all male students is compulsory.

The Army has the largest ROTC program, extending even into more than 300 secondary schools. Two Army programs are conducted at the secondary school level: the Junior ROTC program and the National Defense Cadet Corps, both established in 1916. The Army supports the Junior ROTC by providing instructors, uniforms, and equipment for all cadets. In the National Defense Cadet Corps program, the Army provides training materials, including textbooks, but uniforms are provided by the cadets or by the school system, and instructors are paid and employed by the schools.[13]

The Army's ROTC program is designed to provide officers for both the Reserve and the active-duty forces. The Navy conducts two programs: the Regular ROTC program, known as the Holloway Plan, which offers substantial scholarships and is designed specifically as a source of Navy and Marine Corps active-duty officers; and the Contract ROTC program, designed to procure officers for the Reserve force. The Air Force program is wholly oriented to procuring officers for the active force. The cost per commissioned graduate in the ROTC program in 1963 was: Army $3950, Navy Regular $8913, Navy Contract $3298, and Air Force $6056.[14]

Although the curriculums of the Service ROTC programs vary, they can be characterized as supplementary, or auxiliary, to other subjects the student may be taking in his institution, and are generally patterned in emphasis and content on the professional military instruction given in the service academies. Typically, the ROTC cadet takes some four hours of classroom instruction each week,

---

[12] *Reserve Officers Training Corps Program, op. cit.,* p. 7. Lyons and Masland, *op. cit.,* p. 249. *The Federal Government and Education,* H. R. Document No. 159. Presented by Mrs. Edith Green, Chairman of Special Subcommittee of the House Committee on Education and Labor (Washington, D.C.: USGPO, 1963), pp. 93–94, 149–50.

[13] *Department of Defense Appropriations for 1964: Part 4,* Hearings before a Subcommittee of the House Committee on Appropriations, 88th Congress, 1st Session, pp. 316–17.

[14] *Reserve Officers Training Corps Program, op. cit.,* p. 7.

supplemented by one hour of drill and ceremonies, and a summer camp or summer cruise of four weeks.

At the original suggestion of the Air Force, and patterned somewhat on the Navy's Holloway Plan, the Congress passed legislation sponsored by the Department of Defense which reduces the cadet workload in military subjects measured in class hours, eliminates drill during the academic year, reduces the number of institutions offering the four-year program, and provides a small number of scholarships for students in the last two years of college.

Each service has a civilian ROTC advisory panel, made up of representatives from colleges and universities in which ROTC units are located.

Direct commissioning programs. The services commission, directly from civil life, certain qualified specialists—chiefly physicians, dentists, veterinarians, nurses, lawyers, and chaplains. Navy medical personnel and chaplains serve the needs of the Marine Corps in their respective specialties. The U.S. Public Health Service details professional medical specialists to serve with the Coast Guard. Line officers in the Marine Corps and in the Coast Guard who came into their Service with legal training, or who acquired it on their own after being commissioned, serve as legal officers from time to time but not primarily.

The Coast Guard uses direct commissions to obtain some pilots who have completed Navy or Air Force flight-training programs, and also offers commissions to personnel of the Merchant Marine who have served at least four years as licensed officers on board vessels of the United States.

These various kinds of auxiliary specialists, all of whom have already completed their first professional education or training programs, report for duty with their commissions already awarded, or they are awarded these commissions immediately upon reporting. The services provide brief orientation courses of from three to nine weeks, designed to indoctrinate these specialists in their duties and responsibilities as commissioned officers and to give them some insight into the customs of the service, as well as instruction relating to the practice of their specialties in a military environment. If these specialists elect to become career officers, extensive postgraduate specialized schools, courses, seminars, and other programs are available to them. These brief orientation programs are condensations of academy curriculums. Of all officers reporting for active duty, those with direct commissions have probably the least professional military instruction.

The specialties of law, medicine, dentistry, and nursing offer opportunities for qualified women to become commissioned officers.

Aviation cadet programs. During World War II, and for some time thereafter, aviation cadet programs were a principal means of entry into flying training for the Navy, the Marine Corps, the Coast Guard, and the Air Force, and as shown in Table 7, many officers now on active duty in these services received their commissions through these programs. The Air Force plans that, beginning in 1965, only commissioned officers will enter flying training, and the aviation cadet program will be discontinued.

In the Army, commissioned officers of all ranks may enter flying training, yet flying is not considered an officer's occupational specialty but rather a collateral skill. Military personnel who are at least high school graduates, who wish to become Army warrant officer aviators, and who qualify for training, are given the rank of staff sergeant for the duration of the forty-week flying training period, then are issued warrants when they complete the program.[15] All flying training in the Army is conducted at Fort Rucker, Alabama.

The Navy and the Marine Corps have aviation cadet programs for men who have completed at least two years of college work. These eighteen-month precommissioning programs are given at Pensacola, Florida, and Corpus Christi, Texas. The first phases of professional military education are given in conjunction with flying training. The Navy has programs for flight-crew personnel other than pilots and for aviation ground-support personnel that lead to a commission, but these two programs are given in connection with Navy Officer Candidate Schools, discussed in the following section. The Navy operates pilot-training programs for young commissioned officers from its own service, from the Marine Corps, and from the Coast Guard.

Officer Candidate Schools (OCS). In the past, in peacetime,

---

[15] Warrant officers occupy a unique place in the hierarchy of military rank: between the enlisted and commissioned grades. Although they enjoy certain officer privileges, they are restricted in the degree to which they can supervise and command. Essentially, they are specialists. They are not subject to as frequent rotation and reassignment as are noncommissioned officers and junior commissioned officers.

OCS was considered primarily as the avenue to commissioned rank for the enlisted man with little formal college education but with wide experience and with demonstrated skill and capacity for leadership in a military environment. Developments in the technical complexity of weapon systems and the resulting skill structure of the officer corps have made college graduation or its equivalent practically mandatory for admission to OCS.

It is still possible for an outstanding enlisted man in the Army or the Marine Corps who is not a college graduate to go to OCS. This practice, however, is now the exception rather than the rule.

College graduates now enter OCS directly from civilian life and from the enlisted ranks. The Navy and the Marine Corps also have OCS programs for undergraduates. These programs extend over two summer training periods of eight weeks each, and students are commissioned after they graduate from college. These programs, which are special kinds of Officer Candidate Schools, are known in the Marine Corps as the Platoon Leaders Course (PLC), and in the Navy as the Reserve Officer Candidate (ROC) program. Both these services also have OCS programs open to college graduates, and the Navy, as mentioned above, has flying-training programs related to two of its OCS programs for aviation personnel other than pilots. With the exception of the Coast Guard, all services admit women to OCS programs.

The Navy and the Air Force each have a specially designed subsidized college program leading to a commission for enlisted personnel. The Navy Enlisted Scientific Education Program (NESEP) sends qualified enlisted personnel to a civilian college for four years. The Airman Education and Commissioning Program (AECP) of the Air Force selects qualified enlisted personnel who have at least thirty semester hours of transferable college credit, and sends them to college for as much as two years. In both programs the enlisted men attend OCS after college graduation.

The OCS programs are from three to four months long; they vary according to the amount of military background the officer candidate brings to the school. The Army has three Officer Candidate Schools: at Fort Benning, Georgia, at Fort Sill, Oklahoma, and one for women at the Women's Army Corps Center at Fort McClellan, Alabama. The Navy's schools are at Newport, Rhode Island; the Marine Corps school is at Quantico, Virginia; the Coast Guard school is at Yorktown, Virginia; and the Air Force operation, known as Officer Training School, is in San Antonio, Texas.

The curriculums of these schools vary. The Army and the Marine Corps programs for male officers stress instruction in the tactics and leadership of small units, weapons training, as well as rigorous standards of physical conditioning. As is true of the other programs leading to a commission, the professional military aspects of the school are patterned on those taught at the service academies.

The length of time devoted to professional military education and training in the various commissioning programs varies from very little, in the case of the direct commissioning programs, to the longer periods spread over four years at the academies and in the ROTC programs.

Specialized-Training Programs

A few officers enter the services with specific skills or vocations that are directly related to their military careers. These are officers who are directly commissioned in medicine, law, religion; those who enter through aviation cadet programs and become pilots or navigators before being commissioned; and a relatively small number of skilled enlisted men who enter through officer candidate and officer training schools. The typical newly commissioned officer, however, lacks such a usable skill or vocation and requires fairly extensive formal training and specialized education before he becomes useful in the various officer occupational areas, groups, and subgroups of the services. The amount of education and training he needs will depend upon the career occupational area he chooses, or in which he is placed, and its similarity to his major field of study as an undergraduate. For example, a qualified civil engineer, who is placed in the engineering occupational area will need considerably less training and education than an English major who enters aviation, intelligence, or some other unrelated field. Regardless of the occupation area in which he is placed, the new military officer has begun a career which will consist largely of formal and informal training and education, all of which is concerned directly or indirectly with preparation for war.

Commissioned occupational structure. Each of the services has, over the years, developed its own system of classifying the occupational areas, groups, and subgroups or specialties in which its officers serve. These systems are described in detail in service classification manuals and related documents.[16] Taken as a whole, they provide a means of classifying and coding the skills and levels of competency of individual officers, of identifying and describing positions in the organizations, and of matching individuals with positions.

TABLE 9

SUMMARY OF OFFICER OCCUPATIONAL CLASSIFICATION SYSTEMS
OF THE SERVICES

Service	Occupational Areas	Occupational Groups	Occupational Subgroups	Code
Army	10 Major occupational groups	None	397 Military occupational specialties	MOS: Military Occupational Specialty Code
Navy	10 Major occupational fields	75 Major groupings	1639 Billet classifications	NOBC: Navy Officer Billet Code
Marine Corps	34 Occupational fields	None	93 Military occupational specialties	MOS: Military Occupational Specialty
Coast Guard	7 Occupational fields	66 Groups or specialties	740 Billet classifications	MDC: Military Duty Code
Air Force	15 Career areas	40 Utilization fields	187 Air Force specialties	AFSC: Air Force Specialty Code

Table 9 gives a summary description of the classification systems used by the five services. Analysis of the classification manuals of each of the services shows that the differences in the numbers of occupational areas, groups, and subgroups or specialties among the services are chiefly the results of different methods of classification rather than of real differences in the complexity of the mission to be performed. For example, the manuals of the Navy and the Coast

---

[16] "Manual of Commissioned Officer Occupational Specialties," *Army Regulation 611-110;* "Billet and Officer Designator Codes," *Bureau of Naval Personnel Instruction 1210.4C;* "Manual of Navy Officer Billet Classifications," *NavPers 15839;* "Marine Corps MOS Manual," *NavMc 1008-PD;* "Officer Career Patterns," *United States Coast Guard Commandant Instruction 1040.1;* "Officer Classification Manual," *Air Force Manual 36-1.*

Guard list a total of more than 2300 different specialties, but those
of the Air Force and the Army combined list fewer than 600 specialties. The Marine Corps lists thirty-four occupational *areas* while
the other services list from seven to fifteen.

The methods of classification of the services are different, apparently, because they were developed by different people who had
little or no reason and probably no desire to coordinate their work.
Each system evolved during a period when the services were more
distinctly separate from one another than they are now. Because of
the changes that have taken place in modern warfare, calling for
greater unification of effort among the services, a standardized
method of classification would be more useful today than it was
some years ago. Although there is no standard classification plan
for the Armed Forces as a whole, the Office of the Secretary of Defense is developing various procedures (including the conversion
tables mentioned in Chapter II) to bring about a larger degree of
uniformity in nomenclature.

The following list provides a general notion of the major occupational areas in which officers of the services will be engaged during their careers, and further illustrates the different methods of
classification.

Major Occupational Areas for Officers
of the Army, Navy, and Air Force

1. *Command and Combat*
   Army Occupational Group: Command and Combat
   Navy Occupational Field: Naval Operations
   Air Force Career Areas: (a) Commander and Director
                                 (b) Operations

2. *Personnel*
   Army Occupational Groups: (a) Administrative, Executive, and Training
                                     Services
                                 (b) Welfare and Special Services
   Navy Occupational Field: Personnel
   Air Force Career Area: Administration

3. *Medical*
   Army Occupational Group: Medical, Dental, and other Health Services
   Navy Occupational Field: Medical and Dental
   Air Force Career Area: Medical

4. *Materiel, Logistics, and Transportation*
   Army Occupational Groups: (a) Procurement, Supply, Maintenance, and
                                     Repair Services
                                 (b) Communication and Transportation
   Navy Occupational Field: Supply and Fiscal
   Air Force Career Area: Materiel

5. *Comptroller*

Army Occupational Group:	Fiscal, Accounting, and Budgeting
Navy Occupational Field:	Supply and Fiscal
Air Force Career Area:	Comptroller

6. *Scientific*

Army Occupational Group:	Professional, Subprofessional and Scientific Services
Navy Occupational Field:	Sciences and Services
Air Force Career Area:	Scientific and Development Engineering

7. *Engineering*

Army Occupational Group:	Professional Engineering and Related Technical Services
Navy Occupational Fields:	(a) Shore Construction Engineering
	(b) Electronics Engineering
	(c) Weapons Engineering
	(d) Naval Engineering
Air Force Career Areas:	(a) Electronics and Maintenance Engineering
	(b) Civil Engineering
	(c) Scientific and Development Engineering

8. *Security and Intelligence*

Army Occupational Group:	Protective, Intelligence, and Investigative Services
Navy Occupational Fields:	(a) Sciences and Services
	(b) Personnel
Air Force Career Areas:	(a) Security
	(b) Intelligence

9. *Legal and Chaplain*

Army Occupational Group:	(a) Professional, Subprofessional, and Scientific
	(b) Welfare and Special Services
Navy Occupational Fields:	(a) Sciences and Services
	(b) Personnel
Air Force Career Areas:	(a) Legal
	(b) Chaplain

10. *Public Relations*

Army Occupational Group:	Welfare and Special Services
Navy Occupational Field:	Sciences and Services
Air Force Career Area:	Information

The various occupational specialties are grouped into ten major areas. This list is intended to contain all, or nearly all, the principal occupational categories of the services. For each major occupational area, the appropriate Army occupational groups, Navy occupational fields, and Air Force career areas are listed. The Coast Guard and the Marine Corps have not been included. The classification system used by the Coast Guard is quite similar to that of the Navy. Most of the thirty-four occupational fields of the Marine Corps could be placed within the major occupational groups of the Army.

With approximately 35,000 officers entering the Armed Forces each year and requiring varying degrees of training and special education in at least one of the ten major occupational areas, it is easy to understand the enormity of the training task facing the Armed Forces.

Officer classification.   A manual of each of the services gives a complete description of all specialties in which an officer may serve, including the duties and responsibilities and the prerequisites for service in a particular specialty. As noted in Table 9, the subgroups or specialties in all of the services are coded. During his career, each officer is awarded one or more codes to indicate his qualifications to serve in a number of specialties.

These codes are known as the Military Occupational Specialty (MOS) codes in the Army and the Marine Corps, and—in the other services—as the Navy Officer Billet Code (NOBC), the Coast Guard Military Duty Code (MDC), and the Air Force Specialty Code (AFSC). Generally, they consist of four digits which identify the major occupational areas, the group within the area, and the specialty within the group. In some instances, the digits in the code are used to indicate the military rank of the officer required to fill a given position and the level of the position within an organization. In addition, certain letter or numerical prefixes and suffixes are used to define further the qualifications of an officer or the requirements of a position. The usefulness of these codes in personnel assignment procedures involving automatic data processing systems is obvious.

In addition to describing each specialty and the code associated with it, the service manual gives examples of the positions for which an officer having the code is qualified, the related civilian jobs (using the *Dictionary of Occupational Titles* codes and titles), and the education and experience required or desirable to become fully qualified in the specialty.

Specialty-training programs.   The pattern of the education and training of the typical military career officer, from the commissioning programs through the specialty-training and education programs to the more advanced professional military education programs, is similar to the shape of an hour glass. As described in Chapter II, undergraduate commissioning education is relatively broad in scope. The military education (to be described in Chapter IV) which the officer will receive later in his career is also of a broad and general professional nature. Specialized training and education, representing the narrow waist of the hour glass, takes place in the early years of the officer's career, after he has been commissioned.

The school systems of the five services, described in Chapter II with respect to the training of enlisted men, are also used for the formal training of officers. The courses of instruction for officers, however, are almost always separate from those for enlisted men. They are broader in scope, more complex, usually longer, and predicated upon a higher level of responsibility and educational background.

Army. The more formal specialized training of the typical Army officer is given during the first eight years of service and consists essentially of two phases. Soon after the second lieutenant is commissioned, he attends an orientation course of eight to ten weeks, usually conducted in the various branch service schools. Depending upon the branch to which he is assigned, he may attend the Armor School, the Artillery School, the Infantry School, or any other of the branch service schools operated by the Army. Although the Army regards these as general service schools, they are specialized in the sense that each is designed to meet the needs of a particular branch. Each of them, however, provides general professional education that will be useful to the officer no matter which branch he is assigned to. Thus these schools not only provide specialized training but also lay the basis for the professional military education to be described in more detail in Chapter IV.

After completion of the Orientation Course, the officer is assigned to duty with his branch. Officers in the Military Police Corps, Chemical Corps, Ordnance Corps, Transportation Corps, Quartermaster Corps, Adjutant General Corps, and Finance Corps are detailed to one of the combat branches for their first two years of service in order to experience the combat soldier's needs and problems. At least one year is spent in a rifle company or comparable unit.

After about five years of service, the typical officer, by now a captain, enters the officer career course of his particular branch. The course lasts approximately one academic year and is attended by all career officers of the branch. It consists largely of subjects peculiar to the particular branch, but also includes training applicable to any branch of the Army.

The Army operates a number of specialist schools dealing with the fields of security, civil affairs, aviation, information, intelligence, foreign languages, and others. An officer may attend these schools at any point in his career, depending upon the requirements of his branch or the particular assignments he has received. The officer may be also selected to attend a civilian or military institution for the purpose of obtaining a degree in a special field.

Navy. The more formal specialized training the majority of Naval line officers receive during the first ten years of their careers consists of two major phases. Within the category of line officers, there are the three major areas of specialization: surface vessels, submarine, and naval aviation.

The newly commissioned ensign in the surface-vessels area is assigned to the fleet. He is trained by on-the-job methods, by attending relatively short collateral courses conducted by fleet training commands ashore, and by taking correspondence courses. The object of these is to qualify him for the next higher position or billet. The young officer is rotated through the various departments of the ship, such as gunnery, engineering, communications, and operations. This training is designed to give him a thorough understanding of the organization and operation of a ship at sea. During this first phase, the officer may attend the six-month Destroyer School at Newport, Rhode Island.

Naval flight training normally requires about eighteen months to achieve basic proficiency and is followed by operational assignments to the air arm of the fleet on an aircraft carrier or at a shore-based Naval air station attached to the fleet. Basic Naval flight training takes place at Naval air stations in Pensacola, Florida, and Corpus Christi, Texas.

Training for the submarines begins with a six-month course at the Submarine School at New London, Connecticut, that consists of classroom and practical exercises to qualify the officer in submarine operations. It includes a basic knowledge of engineering applicable to submarines, the operation of submarines, and the use of submarine armaments. Training submarines are attached to the school, and experience in submerged and surface operations, as well as in submarine tactics and strategy, are included as part of the course.

In addition, the Navy provides technical and collateral instruction at ten major centers located on the east and west coasts of mainland United States. Approximately 40 per cent of newly commissioned officers participate before reporting to the fleet. Other officers participate in refresher training in preparation for additional tours of duty at sea or ashore. Literally hundreds of courses are given, each usually less than six months long. They include such subjects as civil engineering, intelligence, air traffic control, communications and electronics, transportation, military justice, cryptography, and a host of others.

During the second phase of specialty training, Naval officers with about six to ten years of service may take advanced courses in any of the specialty-training programs, depending upon Naval requirements and the individual's own estimate of the training he needs for his specialty. Within his specialty, the Naval officer has a large responsibility for planning his career; he himself indicates annually the kinds of collateral training and experience that are most appropriate for his specialty. Keeping in mind the needs of the service and the recommendation of the individual, the Bureau of Naval Personnel makes assignments.

The second phase also includes much of the training given at the Naval Postgraduate School in Monterey, California, and in civilian colleges and universities. (These activities are discussed in a later section of this chapter.)

Marine Corps. Upon receiving his commission, each Marine officer, with the exception of those who will become Marine aviators, attends the Basic Marine Corps School at the Marine Corps Educational Center (Marine Corps Schools) at Quantico, Virginia. The aviators take their flying training at the Navy Flying School at Pensacola, Florida. Immediately following the completion of flight training, they also attend the Basic Marine Corps School.

Because all Marine officers attend the basic school, it cannot be regarded strictly as a specialty-training program within the Marine Corps. It is specialized in the sense that it is unique to the Marines among all the Armed Forces. It is also in part the first step in professional military education (to be discussed in Chapter IV).

The basic course is designed to train the young Marine officer in leading a rifle platoon, the basic fighting element of the Corps. The course is six months long and, depending upon the needs of the service, there may be as many as five classes per year with overlapping schedules. Each class usually consists of about 400 officers.

Much of the course is devoted to field exercises, with about 12 per cent of the work being done at night. During the course, each officer is given the opportunity to occupy each position in a Marine infantry company and is trained in the tactical use of each weapon used in a Marine infantry battalion.

Insofar as possible, the Marine Corps uses the schools and courses of the other services for the specialized training of its officers. The only specialized school at Quantico is the Communication Officers School, which trains selected junior officers for communications duties in the Fleet Marine Forces. It is a six-month course, specializing in the communications used in amphibious operations. The school also offers a four-week orientation course to familiarize graduates of the basic school with the duties of a communications officer in the infantry battalion of a Marine division. As previously mentioned, the Marine aviator receives his specialized training at the Naval Air Station at Pensacola, Florida. Other examples are the Army's career officer courses, in which Marine officers become fully trained in such fields as intelligence, infantry, artillery, engineering, armor, security, and communication.[17]

Nearly 100 separate courses are used by the Marine Corps to train its specialists. The Coast Guard provides 23; the Army, 40; the Navy, 18; civilian colleges and universities, 11; and 5 are joint courses in which the other services participate.

In addition to the resident schools and courses, the specialist has at his disposal the correspondence courses offered by the Marine Corps Institute as well as the correspondence courses of the other services.

Coast Guard. Until recently, most Coast Guard officers were regarded as general-duty officers capable of assuming the duties of any billet in the Coast Guard except those (relatively few) requiring highly specialized·individuals. These specialists have been generally recruited and already extensively trained to assume their responsibilities. They often come from the enlisted ranks or from the Merchant Marine and the Navy. Promotion to higher grades was essentially restricted to the general-duty officer who had demonstrated satisfactory performance in a well-rounded variety of duties. Satisfactory performance in a specialty was regarded as qualification for

---

[17] "Marine Corps Formal Schools Manual," *MCO P1500.12B*, p. III-1.

promotion to the lower grades but not sufficient for promotion to grades above commander.[18]

As recently as November 1963, the Coast Guard officially recognized that the scope of its activities has become so broad that no one officer is able to cover them adequately. In reality the general-duty officer has had to serve as a specialist in several fields, depending upon the particular needs of the billet in which he happened to be serving. Thus the program of specialty training for the Coast Guard is in a process of considerable expansion that will probably continue for a number of years.[19]

As now visualized by the Coast Guard, the training pattern for line officers will be general for the period of time in which they serve as ensigns or lieutenants (junior grade). Officers will acquire a basic knowledge of the sea, ships, and ship operation. The middle career period, during which the officer serves in the grades of lieutenant through commander, will be the period of specialization. Each officer is expected to specialize in one of six major areas: surface operations, aviation, engineering, merchant marine safety, comptrollership, or personnel administration. Thus, the category of general-duty officer will no longer exist.

To provide the specialty training during this period, the Coast Guard intends to assign the officer to various positions in one of the major areas. The officer will also make use of correspondence courses prepared by the Coast Guard Institute. As required by the Coast Guard, many officers will participate in the training programs of the other services, particularly those of the Navy. Much of the preparation for specialization will be taken at the Naval Postgraduate School in Monterey, California (to be discussed in a later section of this chapter).

Air Force. Officers entering the Air Force from the various commissioning sources, whether they are Regulars or Reservists, usually begin their careers with a training program leading to qualification in one of the 187 Air Force specialties. Throughout the development of the Air Force, a large proportion of officers have entered flying training to become qualified as pilots, navigators, or as other specialists in the combat and operations career area. The

---

[18] Officer Career Patterns," *United States Coast Guard Commandant Instruction 1040.1*, p. 1.

[19] *Ibid.*, p. 2–3.

rest have become trained in one of the specialties in the other career areas.

Those completing some form of flying training become classified as *rated* officers; the others are termed *nonrated*. Although all officers, with the exception of those in the medical and chaplain career areas, are line officers, traditionally the rated officer has enjoyed a status similar to that of the Naval unrestricted line officer and the general-duty officer of the Coast Guard. With the Air Force's major emphasis upon the airplane as a weapon system, the rated officer has had opportunities for a wider variety of assignments with higher levels of prestige than the nonrated officer.

With the advent of the missile as an increasingly important type of weapon system, the role of the rated flying officer is likely to diminish in the future. Flying duty, however, will continue to be an important part of the Air Force for many years to come. Personnel projections into the 1970's indicate a continuing need for navigators. The demand for new pilots is likely to decrease in the middle and late 1960's, but pilot duty will probably continue to be a strong area of specialization in the foreseeable future.[20]

Flying-training schools of the Air Force are operated by Air Training Command (ATC), with headquarters at Randolph Air Force Base, Texas. If the officer is able to meet the physical and mental requirements, he goes to one of several bases for preflight, primary, and basic training. This consolidated fifty-five-week flying training course includes 262 hours of flying, 430 hours of classroom instruction in flying, and 329 hours of instruction required of any junior Air Force officer.[21] The fifty-five weeks of training costs $82,400 per pilot.[22]

When he completes preflight, primary, and basic flight training, the officer receives his wings and is a qualified, or undergraduate, pilot. After he is thus qualified, he goes to graduate or combat-training schools operated by the Tactical Air Command, the Strategic Air Command, and the Air Defense Command. There he receives instruction in fighter, bomber, and fighter-interceptor aircraft,

---

[20] *The Air Force as a Profession* (Maxwell Air Force Base, Ala.: Air Force ROTC, January 1963), p. 116.

[21] *Ibid.*, p. 117.

[22] *Department of Defense Appropriations for 1965: Part 1,* Hearings before a Subcommittee of the House Committee on Appropriations, 88th Congress, 2nd Session, p. 290.

and becomes completely qualified for cockpit duty in a tactical organization. This training phase requires an additional six to eight months, it costs as much as $0.5 million per pilot,[23] according to unofficial estimates.

If the officer is selected for navigator training, he will be sent to one of several Air Training Command bases for a twelve-month undergraduate course consisting of 160 hours of flying training, 687 hours of navigation instruction on the ground, and 565 hours of officer training. The program of instruction includes such subjects as radar, astronomy, mathematics, aircraft instruments, navigation, electronics fundamentals, and airmanship.

Upon completion of the undergraduate course, the navigator is usually sent to a more highly specialized thirty- to forty-week advanced course, after which he may be assigned to duty with an operational unit having a mission such as air refueling, transport, air rescue, or troop carrying. Later he may take even more advanced courses to become specialized in all-weather interception, electronic warfare, and radar bombardment.[24]

For the new officer who will not become rated, literally hundreds of courses are conducted by the Air Training Command to help him to become qualified in a specialty. These courses are considerably shorter and less expensive than the flight-training courses. They may be as short as a few days or as long as a full academic year. For career purposes, the longer courses tend to serve the nonrated officer in much the same manner as the flight-training courses serve the rated officer. Nearly all of the officer training courses conducted by the Air Training Command are also open to rated officers. Unlike the rated officer, the nonrated officer may acquire several months of duty experience on the job before he is selected to attend a training command course.[25]

---

23 *Ibid.,* p. 284. Francis V. Drake, "We've Got the Planes, What about the Men?" *Readers' Digest,* 83, 489 (February 1963), 114. Pilot training is the most expensive and hazardous of all service specialized-training programs. As noted in Table 1, the annual amount requested for all service flying training was $726 million. In 1964–65, the annual pilot-training rate was 1500 in the Army, 1700 in the Navy (including Marine Corps and Coast Guard pilot-training requirements), and 1700 in the Air Force. Hearings on Military Posture and H. R. 9637, before the House Committee on Armed Services, 88th Congress, 2nd Session, p. 7077.

24 *The Air Force as a Profession, op. cit.,* p. 118.

25 "USAF Formal Schools Catalog," *Air Force Manual 50-5:* Part III, *passim.*

Like the other services, the Air Force has an extensive program of specialized education conducted in its own Institute of Technology and in civilian institutions to prepare its officers in a variety of specialties.

Specialized Education Programs

Over and above the highly complex *training* programs designed to prepare officers for their specialties, the Armed Forces have a number of programs that might be called *specialized education*. These programs consist of high-level courses, often at the graduate level, and are conducted in degree-granting institutions in both the military and civilian establishments. Although distinction is made between specialized training and specialized education, many of the specialty-training courses are also at a high level, often requiring a bachelor's degree as a prerequisite. The specialized education programs presented here, however, are sufficiently different to be discussed separately.

The military institutions primarily concerned with specialized education are the Naval Postgraduate School at Monterey, California, and the Air Force Institute of Technology at Wright-Patterson Air Force Base, Ohio, a constituent part of Air University.

Naval Postgraduate School. The Naval Postgraduate School has had a long and interesting history.[26] It began in 1904, when a small group of officers were enrolled in a marine engineering curriculum at the Naval Academy at Annapolis. The success of this course led to the establishment of the School of Marine Engineering in 1909, which was designated the Postgraduate Department of the U.S. Naval Academy in 1912. Except for a period during World War I, when it was discontinued, the school remained at Annapolis until it was established at Monterey, California, during the period 1948–51. Between 1912 and 1961, various curriculums, programs, and schools were added to the complex. A reorganization in 1962 resulted in the combination of the separate schools into one, with the academic programs being put under the dual control of a Naval director and a civilian dean.

Today's students are grouped into the curricular programs of aeronautical engineering, electronics and communications engineer-

---

[26] *United States Naval Postgraduate School Catalogue for 1963–64* (Monterey, Calif.), pp. 10–12.

ing, ordnance engineering, naval engineering, environmental sciences, naval management and operations analysis, one-year science, and general line and baccalaureate. Within these areas the student follows a common core program for at least half of the period of residence.

Faculty members are assigned to one of eleven departments covering the areas of engineering, mathematics and physical sciences, management, naval warfare, social sciences, and humanities. About two thirds of the faculty are civilians; the rest are Naval officers.

The programs of the Postgraduate School include: engineering and scientific education leading to specific bachelor's degrees, master's degrees, and doctorates; management education leading to the master's degree; undergraduate education leading to a bachelor's degree; and Navy professional education which may lead to an officer's selection for a two- or three-year engineering or science curriculum for advanced degrees. The Postgraduate School is authorized to confer bachelor's degrees, master's degrees, or doctorates in engineering or related fields and is accredited by the Western College Association and the Engineers Council for Professional Development.

Periods of residence vary from one to three years, depending upon the program being taken. In addition to the courses taken in residence at the Postgraduate School, considerable use is made of civilian colleges and universities to finish programs begun at the Postgraduate School or to provide complete programs leading to advanced degrees.[27]

> In 1961, some 287 graduates were awarded baccalaureate degrees, 175 were awarded master's degrees, and one received his doctorate. Expenditures for the school totaled $14.051 million for 1752 students.[28]

The increasing importance of competence in a technical specialty is indicated by a recent statement by the Chief of Naval Personnel:

> We are placing much more emphasis on specialization in the Navy today than we have in the past. In other words, the so-called rounded career is no longer as important as the officer's specialization or his subspecialization. We are now requiring all officers to have a subspecialization of some sort. All unrestricted line officers,

---

[27] *Ibid.*, p. 53.
[28] *The Federal Government and Education, op. cit.*, p. 59.

such as I am, have a primary specialty: warfare at sea. Naval warfare. That is my prime specialty. My second specialty, my sub-specialty . . . is communications. I am a postgraduate in communications. I specialized in communications during my younger years until I was able to get excommunicated. But each officer, today, is going to be required to have a subspecialty. Now, it could be in strategic planning, . . . political military policy, . . . management, [or] . . . international relations. But mostly it is going to be in technical areas like communications, ASW [Antisubmarine warfare] or missilry. . . . I tell each selection board today . . . that they are not to consider the well-rounded background as important as how well a man has performed and the degree of specialization he has achieved in something other than his naval warfare specialty.[29]

Air Force Institute of Technology. The history of what is now the Air Force Institute of Technology (AFIT) dates back to World War I, when an Army and Navy School of Aeronautical Engineering was opened at the Massachusetts Institute of Technology.[30]

This school closed after graduating two classes. In 1919, however, the Air School of Application was established at McCook Field near Dayton, Ohio. In 1920 it was redesignated the Air Service Engineering School. Students were instructed by specialists assigned to McCook Field.

In 1927 the school was transferred to Wright Field at Dayton, Ohio, along with the expanded engineering and test facilities of McCook Field. It was then renamed the Air Corps Engineering School. It remained in operation until shortly after the beginning of World War II, when classes were suspended. In 1944 it was reopened to conduct short courses to meet emergency needs.

At the close of World War II, a survey of the officer corps indicated a lack of educational attainment and insufficient technical capability among Army Air Force officers. Consequently, the Engineering School was reopened and expanded to form the Army Air Forces Institute of Technology. When the Air Force became a separate service in 1947, the school was renamed the Air Force Institute of Technology. In 1950 it was placed under the command jurisdiction of Air University. At present, the Institute consists of three schools: the School of Engineering, the Civil Engineering Center, and the School of Systems and Logistics. The Institute was

[29] *Department of Defense Appropriations for 1965: Part 1, op. cit.,* p. 195.
[30] *Air University Air Force Institute of Technology Catalogue, 1963–65* (Wright-Patterson Air Force Base, Ohio), pp. I-6–7.

selected by the Department of Defense to operate the Defense Weapons System Management School established in September 1964. The mission of this new school is to develop in officers and civilians from all services the skills required in managing the acquisition of complex, costly, and high-priority weapon systems.

In addition, the Institute administers the Air Force programs in civilian colleges and universities. Each year approximately 4000 students enter programs under the jurisdiction of the Institute.

The School of Engineering and the School of Systems and Logistics are accredited and, like the Naval Postgraduate School, are authorized by Congress to grant baccalaureate and advanced degrees. The accrediting associations are the North Central Association of Colleges and Secondary Schools and the Engineers Council for Professional Development.[31]

The Institute's degree programs are set up largely for the purpose of giving advanced degrees in areas of importance to the Air Force. The resident School of Engineering conducts a small undergraduate program. All courses in the Civilian Institutions Program are directed toward meeting requirements for advanced degrees.

Officers usually enroll in AFIT resident and civilian institutions programs early in their careers. Except for shorter nondegree courses in the Civil Engineering Center and the School of Systems and Logistics, enrollment in the programs is voluntary. The usual procedure is for the student to apply to the Institute for a Certificate of Eligibility. If the Institute review of his educational background shows that he is qualified, he is admitted to a program after Headquarters USAF determines that he can be made available for the period of time required to complete the program.

Specialized courses leading to advanced degrees in the resident programs are: aerospace and mechanical engineering, astronautics, electrical engineering, nuclear engineering, engineering physics, engineering-space physics, reliability engineering, space facilities, and systems management. These courses range in length from one to two years and usually lead to a master's degree. The quotas for fiscal years 1964 and 1965 called for an entry of 293 students into these resident degree programs. In addition, two two-year undergraduate programs in the fields of aeromechanical engineering and electronics are conducted with annual enrollment of thirty students per class.

---

[31] *Ibid.,* p. I-8.

In 1964, the Air Force estimated that in the next ten years, 22,000 officers would require increased technical education in scientific, engineering, and managerial specialties to develop, procure, support, and employ the sophisticated weapon systems that would be developed.[32] In 1963, 25,804 Air Force officers were assigned to positions requiring scientific and engineering knowledge and experience. At the same time, the total Air Force inventory showed only 18,934 officers with baccalaurate or higher degrees in these two fields. The national shortage of this kind of talent will make it difficult for the Air Force to recruit the needed specialists through its commissioning programs. Hence, AFIT programs are necessary in order to provide these kinds of educational programs for career officers.[33]

Civilian institution programs. Over the years the Armed Forces and civilian colleges and universities have enjoyed a relationship that has been marked by an unusually high degree of successful cooperation and coordination. This cooperation has not only resulted in the production of large numbers of officers in the ROTC program, but also in a large amount of defense research which has been of mutual benefit to the Armed Forces and the civilian institutions. The outstanding efforts by civilian institutions to provide off-duty educational opportunities for military personnel are described in detail in Chapter VI.

Each year civilian institutions contribute to the effectiveness of the Armed Forces by providing specialized education for thousands of military officers to meet specific service requirements.

The training of Army personnel at civilian institutions dates from 1868, when special congressional legislation authorized the training of medical officers. The action was followed in 1871 and 1873 by further legislation which granted similar authority to the Chief of Engineers and the Chief of Ordnance, respectively. A more general program was introduced in 1914, at the beginning of World War I, and was later formalized in the National Defense Act of 1920.[34] Currently, the services are allowed to send not more than 8 per cent of their authorized personnel strength to civilian colleges and universities.

---

[32] *Department of Defense Appropriations for 1965: Part 2, op. cit.,* pp. 440–41.
[33] *Ibid.*
[34] *Army Report,* contained in the 1963 unpublished proceedings of the Defense Advisory Committee.

The Army enters about 400 officers per year in civilian institutions; since 1946 some 4000 officers have received postgraduate education in civilian institutions.[35]

In 1963 the Army had students enrolled in 81 U.S. and nine foreign universities for the purpose of providing education to produce officers who could deal effectively with political, economic, scientific, and social problems related to their military duties. A small number specialize in scientific fields to enable them to work effectively with civilian scientists and to direct research and development projects for the Army. Other officers specialize in personnel and industrial management. Civilian institutions are also used by the Army to give language training not provided in Army schools and to provide qualified faculty members for the Military Academy and the Army service schools.[36]

As of April 1963, the Navy had 285 officers in forty-eight civilian institutions taking a wide variety of postgraduate programs including engineering and physical sciences, social sciences, and humanities. The Navy also indicated that it intends nearly to double the number of officers participating in postgraduate programs by 1969.[37]

The Air Force program with civilian institutions is designed to provide advanced education in engineering, physical sciences, arts and social sciences, and management. The largest numbers of students are enrolled in the engineering and physical sciences courses. Also, the program provides for the preparation of Air Force Academy instructors in many fields appropriate to the undergraduate curriculum of the Air Force Academy. During the fiscal year 1965, more than 1300 officers were entered into the programs with 80 cooperative institutions.[38]

An interesting Air Force postgraduate activity is the Strategic Air Command Minuteman Education Program, conducted at five minuteman missile complexes. The instruction at four of these sites is provided by civilian institutions; the faculty of the Air Force Institute of Technology provides instruction at the other. The purpose of the program is to bolster the morale of launch-control officers

35 *Department of Defense Appropriations for 1965: Part 2, op. cit.,* pp. 71, 75.
36 *Army Regulation 350-200.*
37 *Department of Defense Appropriations for 1964,* Hearings before the Subcommittee of the Senate Committee on Appropriations, 88th Congress, 1st Session, on H. R. 7179, pp. 572–73.
38 *Air Force Report,* contained in the 1964 unpublished proceedings of the Defense Advisory Committee.

who are required to spend long and boring hours on the alert at missile sites and to provide education in critical areas without loss of duty time. Courses now included in the program lead to master's degrees in aerospace engineering, business administration, industrial management, or administration. There is also an undergraduate program in mathematics and science. When the program is fully operational, the Air Force intends to have a total enrollment of 800 officers.[39]

The civilian institutions programs of the Marine Corps and the Coast Guard are, of course, smaller than those of the Army, the Navy, and the Air Force. The Marine Corps relies heavily upon the Navy Postgraduate School but has programs in financial management at George Washington University, in management and industrial engineering at Rensselaer Polytechnic Institute, and in personnel administration and training at Stanford University.[40]

The Coast Guard uses both the Naval Postgraduate School and the Air Force Institute of Technology, as well as eight civilian institutions, in such fields as management and administration, naval engineering, civil engineering, aeronautical engineering, electronics engineering, and oceanography.[41]

As was true of ex-servicemen on the GI Bill after World War II, the success of the military officers in their academic pursuits is particularly noteworthy. Not only has the rate of successful completion been high but, as Masland and Radway have observed:

> Not the least important result of the assignment of officers to civilian institutions for graduate study, particularly in the social sciences, has been the contribution they have made to these institutions. We have talked with a considerable number of professors about these men and with very few exceptions they have testified that the officers have made excellent students and have added much to the conduct of seminars and their activities. Moreover, the association of professor and officer has served to increase the mutual understanding between the two professions that was stimulated during World War II.[42]

[39] Ibid.

[40] U.S. Marine Corps Report, contained in the 1963 unpublished proceedings of the Defense Advisory Committee.

[41] U.S. Coast Guard Report, in ibid.

[42] John W. Masland and L. I. Radway, Soldiers and Scholars (Princeton, N.J.: Princeton University Press, 1957), p. 305.

Collateral Training Programs

In addition to the many instructional programs designed to produce specialists, the services conduct a variety of training and educational experiences for both enlisted and commissioned personnel, the object of which is to orient or to train specialists of various ranks and experience to use their skills under certain specialized conditions or circumstances. For the purposes of this monograph, this type of training is termed *collateral instruction* in order to distinguish it from specialist training. These collateral programs do not lead to a MOS, AFSC, or other military specialty designation; rather, the fact that the specialist has had this kind of experience is indicated by a prefix or suffix to his four-digit numerical specialty code.

Many of the conditions for which collateral instruction is designed may be characterized as either physiological, environmental, or tactical in nature.

Examples of physiological conditions that call for collateral training are diving training for intelligence or demolition specialists, training in altitude and explosive decompression chambers for specialists who must perform duties in military aircraft at high altitudes or in tactical submarines, and training in coping with the phenomenon of weightlessness for aviation and astronautic specialists or for other specialists who would be expected to perform duties under similar conditions.

Other special environmental conditions in which military operations take place require the additional training of specialists. One such situation is in the classroom where the specialist acts as instructor. In the Armed Forces, military personnel—both enlisted and commissioned—spend much of their time either being taught or teaching others. The services require specialists to attend instructor-training schools and courses before they are permitted to teach their specialty. These courses are usually about six weeks long and provide intensive practical teaching experience, as well as instruction in methods, evaluation, and educational psychology.[43]

Escape, evasion, and survival in the arctic, jungle, desert, and at

43 "Military Training," *Army Field Manual 21-5;* "Techniques of Military Instruction," *Army Field Manual 21-6;* "Manual for Navy Instructors," *NavPers 16103-B;* "Techniques of Effective Military Instruction," *Marine Corps Educational Center Order P1500. 10B;* "How to Instruct," *Air Force Manual 50-9.*

sea pose special environmental problems for specialists operating in or over these areas and require collateral training.

Duty as civil affairs officer in an occupied foreign area may be temporary, but it requires special training. Competence in the control of damage aboard ship and the disposal of explosive ordnance are skills required in the Navy, the Marine Corps, and the Coast Guard of a wide variety of specialists. Duty as a pilot, in the Army, is not a basic MOS for commissioned officers. It is a skill that is collateral to any commissioned MOS, and officers of all ranks and specialties take collateral pilot training. Career pilots in the Army are warrant officer aviators and civilians on contract.

Many specialists require additional training before they can operate in certain tactical situations. Clandestine and covert operations may call for skills in camouflage, karate, foreign languages, underwater swimming, parachuting, photography, and other special competences. Participation in amphibious landings or in airborne operations necessitates additional training for, among others, medical, chaplain, and intelligence specialists.

Another type of collateral duty that officers may be called upon to perform from time to time is that of military attache in a U.S. embassy abroad, that of military adviser to a foreign government. Or officers may be required to take part in counterinsurgency operations. Languages and associated area education concerning the country to which the officer is to be assigned may require periods of training as long as two years. The Defense Language Institute, with branches in Monterey, California, and in Washington, D.C., conducts courses for all services in over thirty languages, and language courses in civilian colleges and universities and proprietary schools are used as well. Used in this sense, proprietary schools are commercial language schools operated for profit, as contrasted with nonprofit public and privately controlled institutions. The term is found frequently in educational literature. In addition, some officers take language and area instruction at the Foreign Service Institute, operated by the Department of State. The Defense Intelligence School in Washington and the Military Assistance Institute in Arlington, Virginia, offer collateral instruction for military personnel who are going to these foreign assignments.

The Institute operates under the direction of the Assistant Secretary of Defense (International Security Affairs). Its course provides a general coverage of U.S. foreign policy and military strategy as well as an understanding of the organizational relationships among and the functions of the many federal agencies which have responsibilities for military assistance to allied governments. The curriculum includes a detailed study of the country to which the specialist is to be assigned—its history, geography, economics, politics, military forces, and the status of U.S. and Soviet aid programs. In 1964, 8564 military personnel were working abroad in military assistance advisory groups and missions.[44]

Under the Military Assistance Program the services train approximately 25,000 military officers of our allies each year—about 8000 in U.S. schools overseas and some 17,000 in service schools in the United States, at an annual cost of about $80 million.[45] Both the Army and the Air Force operate schools in the Canal Zone for military personnel from Latin America.[46]

Finally, management training is another type of collateral program. As the specialist advances to senior rank and is required to assume larger managerial and supervisory responsibilities, training programs are geared to his needs. A wide variety of fiscal, logistic, transportation, and personnel management courses are used by military specialists, both within the services and in civilian colleges and universities. Because defense expenditures represent such a large proportion of the total federal expenditures, improved management techniques and procedures are stressed at all levels of command. A large increase has also taken place in the degree of centralization of logistic operations and the number of logistic activities that cut across all services. This tendency is expected to continue and to increase.[47] Education and training in joint logistics management is a natural and necessary corollary to this trend in order to provide trained and educated officers and civilian employees to staff these activities.

---

[44] *Department of Defense Appropriations for 1964: Part 3, op. cit.*, pp. 42, 157, 177, 296. See also William R. Kintner, "The Role of Military Assistance," *United States Naval Institute Proceedings*, 87, 3 (March 1961), pp. 76–83.

[45] *The Federal Government and Education, op. cit.*, pp. 110–11.

[46] *Department of Defense Appropriations for 1964: Part 4, op. cit.*, pp. 311–12, 845.

[47] *Study of Management Education and Training: Part 4.* Department of Defense, Special Logistics School Task Group Report (January 18, 1963), pp. IV-6.

CHAPTER IV

Professional Military Education

> War is nothing else than the continuation of state policy by different means.
>
> Karl von Clausewitz, *Vom Kriege* (1831)

Introduction

Professional military education, beyond that offered in the academies, began to develop in the last half of the nineteenth century. The Army Artillery School was established at Fort Monroe, Virginia, in 1867 and was one of the first in the extensive system of professional military schools in the Armed Forces of the United States. The rise of graduate education in the United States, typified by the founding of Johns Hopkins University in 1876, offers an interesting parallel in the history of education. Prior to that time, American graduate students and professors were dependent on European universities for their graduate studies, particularly those in Germany.[1] Developments abroad, including the founding of the famed Prussian Kriegsakademie, also claimed the attention of our military professionals.

> By the mid-1870's it was apparent to any thoughtful soldier that his art was on the threshold of tremendous changes of unpredictable effect. The European conflicts of the 1860's culminating in the Franco-Prussian War of 1870–71 had brought to battlefield application many of the devices which had appeared in only rudimentary form during the Civil War. . . . The scientific and methodical Germans led the way. It was the Germans who developed the general staff system, subsequently imitated by every significant power.[2]

After the Civil War, selected Army and Navy officers were sent on foreign tours of observation. One of these was Major General Emory Upton, a brilliant young Army officer who was a protégé of General William T. Sherman. He was sent on a two-year tour of Asian and European military establishments. On his return, in 1878,

---

[1] Ernest V. Hollis, *Toward Improving Ph.D. Programs* (Washington, D.C.: American Council on Education, 1945), pp. 3–12.

[2] Walter Millis, *Arms and Men: A Study in American Military History* (New York: G. P. Putnam's Sons, 1956), pp. 136–37.

he reported that the Army Academy at West Point was superior to any cadet school he had seen abroad. But he stressed that for American Army officers:

> . . . we have not as yet, except in the artillery, provided them the means of acquiring a theoretical and practical knowledge of the higher duties of their profession.
>
> Abroad it is the universal theory that the art of war should be studied only after an officer has arrived at full manhood, and most governments have established postgraduate institutions for nearly all arms of services, where meritorious officers, from whatever sphere they may enter the Army, may study strategy, grand tactics, and all the sciences connected with modern war.[3]

He included in his report recommendations for the establishment of postgraduate professional schools for the infantry and the cavalry.

Upton's ultimate influence on professional military education, particularly in the Army, was comparable to that of Abraham Flexner's in professional medical education. In addition to Upton, a small group of Army and Navy officers and a few civilians were responsible for great changes in the number, character, and content of postgraduate professional military educational institutions. Prominent among this group were Sylvanus Thayer, Dennis Mahan, Stephen Luce, Tasker Bliss, Alfred Thayer Mahan, Spencer Wilkinson, and Elihu Root.[4] Their efforts culminated in the establishment of the Naval War College in 1884 and the Army War College in 1901.

By the turn of the century the pattern of the professional military educational structure was fairly well established. The next major development was the establishment of the Army Air Corps Tactical School at Langley Field, Virginia, after World War I. Post-World War II developments included the establishment of Air University as the professional educational center for the newly autonomous U.S. Air Force, and the establishment of the Department of Defense

---

[3] Emory Upton, *The Armies of Asia and Europe* (New York: Appleton-Century-Crofts, Inc., 1878), pp. 360–63.

[4] John W. Masland and Lawrence I. Radway, *Soldiers and Scholars* (Princeton, N.J.: Princeton University Press, 1957), pp. 79–86; Samuel P. Huntington, *The Soldier and the State* (Cambridge, Mass.: Belknap Press, 1957), pp. 230–42; Albert N. Gleaves, *Life and Letters of Admiral Stephen B. Luce* (New York: G. P. Putnam's Sons, 1925), *passim;* Spencer Wilkinson, *The Brain of an Army* (London: Macmillan & Co., Ltd., 1890), *passim;* and Albert N. Gleaves, *Thirty-Five Years: 1874–1909* (London: Constable & Co., Ltd., 1933), pp. 258–61.

and the major joint schools in which all the services participate—
the Armed Forces Staff College, the Industrial College of the
Armed Forces, and the National War College.

In his searching analysis of the professional military role in contemporary society, Huntington attempts to identify the unique ex-
pertness of the military officer. He notes that the officer corps
contains many specializations that are also found in civilian life:

> Engineers, doctors, pilots, ordnance experts, personnel experts,
> intelligence experts, communications experts—all these are found
> both within and without the modern officer corps. Even ignoring
> these technical specialists, each absorbed in his own branch of
> knowledge, just the broad division of the corps into land, sea, and
> air officers appears to create vast differences in the functions per-
> formed and the skills required. The captain of a cruiser and the
> commander of an infantry division appear to be faced with highly
> different problems requiring highly different abilities.
>
> Yet a distinct sphere of military competence does exist which is
> common to all, or almost all, officers and which distinguishes them
> from all, or almost all, civilians. This central skill is perhaps best
> summed up in Harold Lasswell's phrase, *the management of vio-
> lence.*[5]

This definition of the military profession has gained considerable
currency, but has not been completely accepted by the services, perhaps because national policy dictates that American Armed Forces
exist primarily to deter war. Also, this generalization may obscure,
in some minds, the important logistic and research and development
managerial aspects of the profession.

A central concern of the military profession involves tactics and
strategy. Tactics has been defined as that branch of military art or
science which deals with the positioning, arranging, and maneuver-
ing of forces in combat, using equipment and weapons, military
persons or units, positive action or passivity—all with the purpose
of achieving in a combat situation some immediate advantage or
ameliorating a disadvantage with force or forces at hand.[6] In contrast, strategy might be thought of as the orchestration of tactics, or
more precisely:

---

[5] Huntington, *op. cit.,* p. 11.
[6] Woodford A. Heflin, (ed.), *The United States Air Force Dictionary* (Maxwell
Air Force Base, Ala.: Air University Press, 1956).

·   The art or science of using such factors as time, space, geography, politics, and trends of events, together with available or potential power, to achieve a previously conceived objective; or the use of these factors to create advantageous conditions for meeting the enemy in combat, either to compel surrender or to achieve some other objective.[7]

Ultimately, the end of strategy is to influence the opponent's decisions.

These definitions or generalizations indicate, at least in broad terms, the content of professional military education—the subject matter the officer must master to be effective. Beyond knowledge of subject matter, however, there are certain attitudes that have historically characterized officership and set it apart. Although imperfectly attained or applied, these attitudes may be best summed up in the motto of the military academy at West Point: "Duty, Honor, Country." The importance of these ideals is found throughout military history and in the best of the contemporary literature, and some appreciation of their relevance is necessary to an understanding of the profession. They cannot be treated in this monograph, but they permeate every level of officer training and education.

Structure of Professional Military Education

Formal training and education for the profession of arms begins in the undergraduate college and may not end until the officer has served more than twenty-five years and has reached the age of forty-five or older. Contrary to popular opinion, the officer, in the beginning stages of his career, knows relatively little about the art and science of warfare, and it will be years before he can be accurately described as being truly professional in the sense that he can deal effectively with complex problems of strategy and tactics, or command and staff.

Analysis of the programs for officers of all the services indicates there are seven possible levels at which professional military education can take place. These levels might be termed in the manner shown in Table 10, which also includes the approximate rank and

---

[7] *Ibid.*

TABLE 10

LEVELS OF PROFESSIONAL MILITARY EDUCATION

Level Program	Equivalent Rank of Average Officer	Aproximate Years of Service
1 Commissioning programs	Cadet	0
2 Initial-training programs	Second Lieutenant	1
3 Career-training programs	Captain	5
4 Command and staff colleges	Major	12
5 Senior service colleges	Lieutenant Colonel	19
6 National and joint colleges	Colonel	22
7 Combined college (NATO)	Colonel	22

TABLE 11

PROFESSIONAL MILITARY EDUCATION PROGRAMS
OF THE ARMED SERVICES

Level	Army	Navy	Marine Corps	Coast Guard	Air Force
1	(Commissioning programs, i.e. academies, ROTC, OCS, and so on)				
2	Branch Schools (Orientation Course)	Surface Submarine and Flying Schools. Officer Special Schools	Basic School	Naval Schools	Pilot-, Navigator-, and Specialty-Training Programs of Air Training Command
3	Branch Schools (Career Course)	Naval Post Graduate School	Junior School	Naval Schools	Air University; Squadron Officer School
4*	Army Command and General Staff College	Command and Staff Course (Naval War College)	Senior School	Other Service Command and Staff Schools	Air University; Command and Staff College
5	Army War College	Naval Warfare Course (Naval War College)	Other Service War Colleges	Other Service War Colleges	Air University; Air War College
6	National War College; Industrial College of the Armed Forces	Same	Same	Same	Same
7	NATO Defense College	Same	Same	Same	Same

* Between the fourth and fifth level specified numbers of officers attend the Armed Forces Staff College at Norfolk, Va.

years of service of the typical officer attending school at a given level. Table 11 shows the programs at each level for each service.

Characteristics of the professional military education structure. At the first two levels—Commissioning and Initial Training Programs—professional military education is conducted in schools and colleges whose primary purpose is other than to provide professional military education. Thus, in these early stages the amount of time spent, and the depth and scope of what has been defined as professional military education, are considerably less than those found at the higher levels. For example, in the commissioning programs conducted in the academies and the undergraduate civilian colleges, the student spends most of his time on formal undergraduate studies and relatively little time on professional military subjects. Likewise, the specialty-training programs at the second level are often more concerned with training leading to a specific MOS or AFSC than they are with broad military education applicable to any military occupational area or specialty.

At each successive level the numbers of students become smaller and smaller. At the first level, for example, there are hundreds of thousands of cadets participating. But only a small percentage of these are commissioned and will attend a school at the second level. Large numbers of those who complete their training at the second level are officers who will leave the service at the end of their initial tours of duty. The third-level schools are reserved almost exclusively for career officers. Selection of the career officers best-qualified for professional military education programs begins, in some cases, at the third level. The Squadron Officer School, the first truly professional military school of the Air Force, graduates only a little more than 50 per cent of the career officers. At the fourth level, Command and Staff, selectivity becomes even greater for all services and only about 1520 of the 343,121 officers on active duty are able to attend school each year at this level. In the senior colleges, the number attending each year is slightly more than 600, which is a fraction of 1 per cent of all active-duty officers. Only 655 senior officers attend the National War College, the Industrial College of the Armed Forces, the Armed Forces Staff College, or the NATO Defense College (the only truly international professional military school).

Because smaller and smaller numbers of officers attend at each successive level, the schools at all levels may be considered terminal for large numbers of officers. For others the schools at a given level are part of a sequence of professional military education. This creates a problem in curriculum development. Each school must provide appropriate instruction for officers who will end their formal professional military education upon graduation, as well as for those officers who will attend a school at the next higher level. To complicate the problem further, some officers who have not attended a lower-level school may be selected to attend school at the next level. In most instances, these officers could not be made available at certain stages of their careers because of operational requirements. During World War II and the Korean conflict, many officers lost their opportunity to attend one or more professional military schools at various levels because they were needed for combat operations. Consequently, there is a degree of duplication in subject matter and coverage among the successive schools within any one of the services.

Few, if any, officers are able to attend school at each of the seven levels of professional military education. If, however, an officer were to receive all available education for his particular service, it would amount to as much as four years or more of what might be considered the graduate-level instruction for his profession. This compares reasonably well with the education required of other professions, such as law, engineering, or teaching. Most successful career officers of the rank of colonel will probably attend professional military school for a total of more than three academic years at various stages of their careers.

Selection for nearly all professional military schools is on an involuntary basis. Because selection tends to be from among the most highly qualified officers at various stages of their careers, very few fail to complete their courses of instruction because of academic deficiency. There are few failures at the lower levels and none at the higher levels of professional military education.

Professional military education is largely a peacetime operation. Many of the programs are drastically reduced or discontinued entirely during periods of war. For example, the Army War College was closed during World War II and was not reopened until 1950.

Curriculums of the Professional Military Schools

The curriculums for each of the professional military schools listed below are described in detail in the catalogs of the respective schools and are not covered here.[8]

United States Professional Military Schools

Army

Branch Service Schools * (Career Course)
Command and General Staff College, Fort Leavenworth, Kansas
War College, Carlisle Barracks, Pennsylvania

Navy

War College, Newport, Rhode Island
    Command and Staff Course
    Naval Warfare Course

Marine Corps

Army Branch Schools (Career Courses **)
Educational Center, Quantico, Virginia
    Basic School
    Junior School
    Senior School

Coast Guard

Other Service Schools, particularly Navy Schools

Air Force

Air University, Maxwell Air Force Base, Alabama
    Squadron Officer School
    Command and Staff College
    War College

Joint Schools

Armed Forces Staff College, Norfolk, Virginia
Inter-American Defense College, Fort McNair, Washington, D.C.
Foreign Service Institute of U.S. State Department, Arlington, Virginia
Industrial College of the Armed Forces, Fort McNair, D.C.
National War College, Fort McNair, D.C.

Combined Schools

NATO Defense College, Paris, France

* There are nineteen Army Branch Service Schools.
** Infantry, Artillery, Engineer, Armor, Ordnance, and Signal Corps Branch Schools.

---

[8] See footnote 20, p. 40.

Foreign Service Schools †

British Imperial Defense College
British Joint Services Staff College
British Joint Warfare Establishment
British Royal Naval Staff College
British Royal Air Force Staff College
British Army Staff College
British Royal Marine Installations and Commands
British Royal Armored Center
Canadian National Defense College
Canadian Army Staff College
Royal Canadian Air Force Staff College
Royal Canadian School of Artillery
Australian Army Staff College
Royal Australian Air Force Staff College
Republic of West Germany General Staff College
French Superior War School
French Naval War School
French Army Staff School
Italian War School
Italian School of Air Warfare
Spanish General Staff School
Spanish Naval War College
Uruguayan Military Institute of Superior Studies
Argentina Command and General Staff College
Indian Defense Services Staff College
Pakistan Army Staff College

† This is a representative list of schools that U.S. Armed Forces officers attend in limited numbers and usually on an exchange basis.

Source: Army Regulation 350-2 NAVPERS 91769-F; Marine Corps MCOP 1500.12B; Air Force Regulation 36-41.

Analysis of the curriculums throughout the seven levels of professional military education suggests the following major areas in which most of the subject matter of all of the services could be classified:

1. *Military strategy, tactics, and employment:* principles of war; military history; basic service doctrine; employment of U.S. forces, employment of unified, specified, and joint commands; impact of technology on tactics and strategy; broad spectrum of warfare; and the potential military uses of space.

2. *National security policy and strategy:* national objectives, development of the national policy role of the Department of Defense, the relation of national security policy and strategy to the economy.

3. *International relations:* alliances and pacts, elements of national power, international power politics, geopolitics, and factors influencing the intensity of war.

4. *Military management:* knowledge of administrative procedures, organization, and functions; principles of staff management; manpower and personnel; intelligence systems; logistics systems; budget and fiscal poli-

cies; and the organization and equipment of combat and support units.

5. *Individual skills:* writing, speaking, techniques of negotiation, problem-solving procedures, and research methods.

Levels of Education

As noted earlier, there tends to be a degree of duplication—at least in the topics covered—throughout the successive levels of professional military education. But considerable differences exist among the levels with respect to the degree of emphasis placed upon the various subjects. For example, the instruction given at the Basic School of the Marine Corps is primarily concerned with the development of leadership characteristics of the second lieutenant, with particular emphasis upon the duties and responsibilities of a rifle-platoon leader. In the Junior School, emphasis is placed upon command and staff duties and the responsibilities associated with amphibious operations involving infantry battalions and regiments, and aircraft squadrons and groups. The Senior School of the Marine Corps, which the officer attends when he has achieved the rank of major or lieutenant colonel, emphasizes doctrine, tactics, and techniques of amphibious warfare involving one or more Marine divisions and aircraft wings.[9] Later in his career the Marine officer may attend one of the senior colleges of the other services, where he will study broader aspects of doctrine and strategy involving combat forces of the Army, the Navy, and the Air Force. Still later, he may attend one of the joint or combined colleges where emphasis is placed upon national and international strategy.

The foregoing example is true in varying degrees of the professional military education systems of the other services. Although no two curriculums of the services are alike, certain generalizations concerning the differences among lower, intermediate and higher levels of professional military education can be made:

1. *Lower levels (first and second).* Here emphasis is placed upon minor tactics involving small military units. Individual skills, with particular attention to leadership characteristics, are stressed. The education tends to be oriented toward the established policies and doctrine of the particular branch or service. It is also likely to be of a highly practical nature and includes a great deal of repetition in order to insure that pro-

---

9 "Marine Corps Formal Schools Manual," *MCO P1500.12B.*

fessional military skills are developed and mastered to the highest possible degree.

2. *Intermediate levels (third and fourth).* At these levels particular attention is paid to larger units such as battalions, groups, wings, divisions, and major commands within a given service. The essence of the intermediate levels of professional military education is to provide an understanding of command and staff procedures, including the history and development of the military staff beginning with the contribution of Gustavus Adolphus in the seventeenth century.[10] It is here that the officer begins serious and scholarly research into the fundamental aspects of his profession. For many officers it will be their first opportunity to develop and write a military staff study, which includes stating a problem, analyzing the multiple factors bearing on the problem, discussing possible solutions, drawing conclusions, and making recommendations to be considered by higher authority. Most of the work at this level is concerned with the application of force within the established doctrine of a given service and established national objectives.

3. *Higher levels (fifth, sixth, seventh).* In the senior service colleges, the officers begin to look critically upon the concepts and doctrine of their own service as well as those of the other services. The problems studied often go beyond the doctrine of one particular service; the problems of unified, specified, and joint commands take on increasing importance. Of particular concern at these higher levels is the doctrine and strategy of the future. The officer is usually required to write a major thesis on an important aspect of the subject matter of the military profession.

The various levels of professional military education are a series of experiences in solving problems of increasing complexity. As weapon systems and related logistic and communication systems grow more and more complex, as the weight of firepower increases, as the spectrum of war widens to include operations in space, and as U.S. relations with other countries become more interdependent, the importance of the professional military education of the officer corps continues to grow.

In 1962 the officers attending the National War College were told:

> Any thoughtful consideration of the scope of military responsibility, and the breadth and depth of the requirements for expertise, should make any self-respecting professional forget his Cold War frustrations in the hard work of acquiring and exercising the expertise which the country expects of the military. . . . expertise in the

---

[10] J. D. Hittle, *The Military Staff: Its History and Development* (Harrisburg, Pa.: The Stackpole Company, 1961).

fields of intelligence and planning, in development of strategies and the design of forces, in combat leadership and the conduct of operations, in training, in establishing doctrine and tactics, in defining requirements, in procurement and stock control, in directing research and development, and in the over-all management and administration of the tremendous resources that have been entrusted to . . . [them] by the American people.[11]

---

[11] An unpublished address to the National War College, by The Honorable Eugene M. Zuckert, Secretary of the Air Force, December 6, 1962.

CHAPTER V

Unit Training

And the Lord said to Gideon, With the three hundred men that
lapped I will deliver you, and give you the Midianites into your hand.
Judges 7:7

Introduction

In the introduction to their discussion of the professions, Carr-Saunders and Wilson explain why they omitted consideration of the church and the army:

> The former is left out because all those functions related to the ordinary business of life, education among them, which used to fall to the church, have been taken over by other vocations. The functions remaining to the church are spiritual, and we are only concerned with the professions in their relation to the ordinary business of life. The army is omitted because the service which soldiers are trained to render is one which it is hoped they will never be called upon to perform.[1]

However laudable this pious hope may be, the fact remains that because the military profession performs its function in a combat situation with relative infrequency, it has a more difficult training and educational problem. Historically, the practice maneuver has been the profession's method of coping with this disadvantage. Today, maneuvers, war games, and other forms of service, interservice, and international training exercises are so important to the Armed Forces, and so relatively costly, that this separate though brief treatment is warranted.

Purposes of Unit Training

In combat, self-confidence is tremendously important, and good training engenders this self-confidence. But, more important, the individual must have confidence in those who command him, those who support him, and, in the final analysis, those on either side of

---

[1] A. M. Carr-Saunders and P. A. Wilson, *The Professions* (Oxford: The Clarendon Press, 1933), p. 3.

him. The purpose of unit training, never fully achieved, is battle readiness—to weld trained specialists, enlisted and commissioned, into an effective whole for a specific mission or for a series of missions and tasks.

The size of the unit may range from a two-man rifle reconnaissance team to a unit consisting of hundreds of thousands of individuals from all services and many nations. Unit training has at least these purposes: to evaluate the effectiveness of education and training programs; to identify potential leaders; to promote combat readiness; to provide practice in combined-arms coordination; to test new doctrine and tactics, weapons, and equipment; and to foster self-confidence.

Other purposes involved in unit training are not significantly related to this study and will be only mentioned here. These relate to the possible political and diplomatic advantages that lie in making visible to allies and potential enemies alike the military posture or capabilities of the nation.

Nature of Unit Training

As a part of its training responsibility, each service conducts unit training apart from its more formal classroom instruction. The Joint Chiefs of Staff are responsible for the joint training of the unified and specified commands. In the Army and the Marine Corps, the central concern in unit training begins with the smooth functioning of the rifle squad. Here, one of the important training tasks is to assure that in combat every man will fire his weapon—even at the risk of attracting enemy fire.[2]

Larger training exercises within the Marine Corps are concerned with amphibious operations in which battalions, regiments, and divisions are landed on a "hostile" shore. Complex unit training exercises within the Army may involve one of the numbered field armies made up of two corps, totaling from 40,000 to 100,000 men and involving Army aviation units, tanks, and ground-to-ground missiles. In Navy training exercises, units may be as small as the crew of a single ship, submarine, or aircraft, or as large as a task force of

---

2 In World War II it was estimated that 75 per cent of American Army infantrymen did not fire or would not persist in firing. S. L. A. Marshall, *Men Against Fire* (New York: William Morrow & Co., Inc., 1947), pp. 50ff.

many surface vessels, submarines, and aircraft. Small-unit exercises in the Air Force might be confined to a single aircraft crew in a tactical operation, a missile-launch crew, or a few planes in a mid-air refueling operation. Large-unit exercises may involve groups, wings, and divisions of fighters and bombers participating in a massive air-strike or air-defense exercise. The unique exercises of the Coast Guard are confined to the operation of small units.

Beyond the unit training activities within each service, still larger joint and combined exercises are conducted which may involve not only unified and specified commands of the United States, but those of other nations as well. Joint exercises involve units of more than one service; combined exercises include units of one or more allied nations.

Unit exercises involve a great number of individuals and units and a great variety of organizations and combinations of weapon systems and equipment. The following examples illustrate the range and variety of these activities.

1. In the jungles of northern Okinawa, the Marine Corps operates a counterguerrilla warfare school. The school was established to provide unit training for the Marine Corps' Third Division troops selected for duty in Vietnam. Every infantry battalion in the Division goes through the school, which stresses self-reliance under jungle conditions.[3]

2. At Glynco, Georgia, the Navy operates a Combat Information Center School. The surface members of an air-defense team stationed in Georgia work with Navy and Marine pilots flying over the Atlantic to perfect all-weather ground-controlled interceptor procedures to counter enemy aircraft or missiles.

3. Off New York harbor a Coast Guard helicopter crew practices routine procedures for the rescue of a downed airman or the crew of a stricken vessel.

4. In the Carribean, Navy destroyers, aircraft, and submarines test new tactics in antisubmarine warfare.

5. An Air Force first lieutenant pilot, with 2500 hours of flying time, reports to a Strategic Air Command Combat Crew Training Squadron for a twenty-two-day training course designed to furnish the minimum operational knowledge necessary to fly the supersonic

---

[3] "Jungle Seminar," *Yank* (1963, special issue), pp. 55–57.

B-52. Later he is one of a six-man crew consisting of pilot, co-pilot, navigator, radar-navigator, electronics countermeasures operator, and gunner. He will practice bomb-runs on preselected targets and mid-air refueling procedures.[4]

6. The Army's Special Warfare Center at Fort Bragg, North Carolina, conducts an exercise—code name WATER MOCCASIN III—in a 2500-square mile area in Georgia. The exercise is the fourth in a series and is designed as the final examination of the Special Warfare School course. The exercise trains U.S. officers, along with 124 officers from seventeen other nations, in each type of guerrilla/counterguerrilla warfare being waged in Vietnam.[5]

7. A fourteen-day unit exercise, known as DESERT STRIKE and involving both the Army and the Air Force, was conducted in a 13 million-acre area along the California-Arizona border in May 1964. It involved over 100,000 men, several hundred tanks and self-propelled guns, 300 Air Force supersonic jet-fighter aircraft, 150 Army planes, and 300 helicopters.

8. Units of all U.S. Armed Forces and Canadian forces, coordinated by the North American Air Defense Command (a U.S. unified command), participate in periodic air-defense exercises. The problem is to test the reaction time and capabilities of American and Canadian defense forces to counter a massive manned bomber and missile attack on the North American continent. One such exercise, conducted in 1962, lasted five and one-half hours and involved Army missile and radar sites in the United States, Canada, and Europe; Navy picket ships and planes; and Air Force bombers and fighter-interceptor aircraft. Some 700 military installations were involved and more than 150,000 servicemen took a direct part, while another 100,000 supported the operation. During the exercise all domestic and foreign commercial flights were cancelled.[6]

9. Since 1961 the NATO level of military operations has conducted three unit exercises of mobile forces made up of units and forces from as many as seven NATO countries. These exercises are designed to test the mechanics of command, communications, and logistics of an international force fighting in an unfamiliar land.

---

4 *Strategic Air Command Manual 51-3.*

5 *Department of Defense Appropriations 1965: Part 2,* Hearings before a Subcommittee of the House Committee on Appropriations, 88th Congress, 2nd Session, p. 146.

6 *The New York Times,* September 3, 1962, p. 1:2.

The exercises have taken troops from temperate climate to the heat of southern Italy and Greece and to the cold and mountainous terrain of Norway.[7]

At the conclusion of maneuvers and other forms of unit training, the services evaluate and hold critiques on the exercise. The results of these evaluations then affect the courses of study of the individual service schools as well as the design of subsequent programs.

Cost of Unit Training

In justifying the need for more military exercises, the Chairman of the Joint Chiefs of Staff has stated:

> The United States has entered into multilateral treaties and bilateral agreements involving over forty countries. All of these agreements create potential military obligations for our forces which may fall due at any time at many different parts about the world. In anticipation of these possible contingencies, our oversea commanders maintain a catalog of some fifty-five major contingency plans which, in their totality, represent a requirement for military forces far in excess of any permanent military establishment which the United States can or should maintain.
>
> We can meet these commitments only by having in central strategic reserve a highly mobile force representing all the services, ready for prompt movement overseas. This kind of readiness can be established and maintained only through repeated rehearsals and maneuvers.[8]

The costs of conducting unit exercises in the Armed Forces are not included in the $3.091 billion reported in Table 1 for individual training and education. From the available literature it has not been possible to estimate the total costs for annual unit training for all of the services. During the fiscal year 1963, however, it was estimated that the Army alone spent nearly $100 million for this purpose.[9] It could be argued that in the absence of general war, the entire defense budget of approximately $50 billion is involved in one way or another with unit training.

---

[7] *NATO's Fifteen Nations*, 8:6 (December 1963-January 1964), 61–68.

[8] *Department of Defense Appropriations for 1964:* Hearings before the Subcommittee of the Senate Committee on Appropriations, 88th Congress, 1st Session, p. 1616.

[9] *Department of Defense Appropriations for 1965: Part 2, op. cit.,* pp. 149–51.

CHAPTER VI

Off-Duty Education

No one will live all his life in the world in which he was born, and no one will die in the world in which he worked in his maturity. For those who work on the growing edge of science, technology, or other arts, contemporary life changes at even shorter intervals. Often only a few months may elapse before something, which previously was easily taken for granted, must be unlearned or transformed to fit the new state of knowledge or practice. In today's world no one can complete an education.

Margaret Mead, "A Redefinition of Education,"
NEA Journal (October 1959)

Introduction

The term *off-duty education* is used to identify nonmilitary courses of study that servicemen pursue on their own initiative. Because the training and educational needs of the service may differ from the educational desires of the individual, these divergent needs may be satisfied in the off-duty program. Apart from a general interest in promoting morale, the services support off-duty education so that individuals may acquire the knowledge and skills that are needed to complete technical courses offered in service schools for military specialists. The services are also interested in encouraging individuals both to complete educational programs that may have been interrupted by military service and to pursue their own intellectual interests. Finally, the general service interest in encouraging the learning of a second language stems from the worldwide deployment of U.S. forces and the contribution that facility in using a second language makes toward better relations with the people of countries in which these forces are stationed.

United States Armed Forces Institute

As indicated in Chapter I, the Deputy Assistant Secretary of Defense (Education) is responsible for establishing plans and policies concerning off-duty education within the Department of Defense. One of the major responsibilities of the Directorate for Education

Programs of this office is the supervision of the United States Armed Forces Institute (USAFI) at Madison, Wisconsin.

USAFI gives military personnel opportunities to continue their education while they are on active duty. It supplies instructional materials and examinations at the high school and college level.

The need to provide educational opportunities for servicemen became apparent early in World War II. With the advice of prominent educators, USAFI began operation on April 1, 1942, using facilities provided by the University of Wisconsin and offering courses purchased from the International Correspondence Schools and from the extension divisions of about seventy colleges and universities. By December 1942, USAFI programs were made available to all services; USAFI was given its present designation in February 1943. At the end of World War II, the decision was made to continue USAFI as a permanent activity of the Department of Defense.[1]

Through USAFI, servicemen are given an opportunity to study subjects to improve their performance as specialists and to prepare themselves for promotion to more responsible jobs in the Armed Forces. They also may prepare themselves for second careers when they retire or leave the Armed Forces.

USAFI offers some 200 high school, college, and technical-vocational correspondence and group-study courses, including courses in twenty-four spoken languages. Forty-three colleges and universities now cooperate in offering correspondence courses through USAFI. Students enroll in these courses through the Institute, after which they deal directly with the cooperating institutions.[2]

USAFI offers a number of tests and testing programs to assess the educational level of the individual servicemen. Many civilian colleges and universities recognize these test results by giving advanced standing equivalent to the level attained.

The estimated operating cost of USAFI for the fiscal year 1964 was $5.379 million.[3] During the previous year, 120,552 new students enrolled in its correspondence courses, 178,885 in group-study courses, and 13,902 in the correspondence courses of participating

---

[1] *USAFI Catalog* (September 1963), 4; Wilbur L. Brothers, "Education in the Armed Forces," *Adult Education,* 9:4 (Summer 1959), 244–48.

[2] *Ibid.*

[3] *Department of Defense Appropriations for 1964: Part 4,* Hearings before the Subcommittee of the Senate Committee on Appropriations, 88th Congress, 1st Session, p. 979.

colleges—a total of 313,339 new enrollments. During this period 769,647 individual tests were scored. The total mail processed during the period exceeded 2.8 million pieces for the third consecutive year.[4] In the exercises commemorating the Institute's twentieth anniversary (in 1962), it was announced that 2 million servicemen had attained high school equivalency certificates or diplomas through USAFI programs. In 1963 the number of college-level correspondence courses exceeded for the first time the numbers of lessons received from enrollees in high school courses.[5]

All USAFI offerings are evaluated by the Commission on Accreditation of Service Experiences (CASE) of the American Council on Education. The Commission is composed of twelve civilian members appointed by the President of the American Council on Education. He is a member ex officio. Representatives of the Office of the Deputy Assistant Secretary of Defense (Education), and of the Army, the Navy, the Marine Corps, the Coast Guard, and the Air Force attend the semiannual meetings of the Commission as consultants and observers.[6]

Recommendations made by CASE on the amount of advanced standing that civilian colleges and universities may grant for USAFI courses are only advisory; the final determination on credit to be granted is made by the individual educational institution. CASE maintains close liaison with the Office of the Deputy Assistant Secretary of Defense (Education), with secondary schools, colleges, and universities, and with regional accreditating associations. CASE has over-all supervision of the USAFI testing program at the high school level and higher.

College Programs

Members of the Armed Forces may also pursue off-duty education through a variety of programs offered by American universities and colleges. These university-extension and adult-education programs are dealt with in other volumes of the Library of Education. Only representative programs of this type are described here.

---

4 *USAFI Activity Report: Calendar Year 1963*, p. vi.
5 *Department of Defense Appropriations for 1964: Part 4, op. cit.*, p. 979.
6 *The Commission on Accreditation of Service Experiences: Purpose, History and Activities* (Washington, D.C.: American Council on Education, n.d.), pp. 1–11.

The University of Maryland conducts predominantly undergraduate educational programs at 138 military centers in Europe, Africa, and the Middle East, at fifty centers in the Far East, and at eight centers in the Atlantic Division (which includes the Azores, Bermuda, Greenland, Iceland, and Newfoundland).[7]

Florida State University has programs on military bases in Puerto Rico and the Canal Zone. Boston University and the University of Southern California both have specialized postgraduate programs at Army and Air Force installations in Germany.

Within the United States, American servicemen attend university resident and extension classes, usually at night, along with other students from the adult civilian community. In addition to these classes, some colleges and universities have programs designed specifically for military personnel. It has been estimated that as many as 200 American colleges and universities have one or more such programs. These classes are conducted on military bases as well as in university-owned facilities. In some instances, certain of these institutions cross state and even regional boundaries to give this service, probably because the local or state institutions are either unable or unwilling to provide it.

In support of these various off-duty programs, in 1964 the services were authorized to pay up to $14.25 per semester hour toward defraying tuition costs. In addition, whenever a member of the Armed Forces gets to the point in his off-duty educational program that he can complete degree requirements by attending the college full-time for one semester or for one academic year, the services are authorized to order him to temporary duty at the institution, and to continue to pay his salary for that period. The serviceman pays the tuition and other fees.

Each service makes an annual report of certain of its educational programs to the DACE committee. What is included in these individual reports is left to each service to decide. These individual service reports are interesting and replete with statistics on various aspects of the training and educational activities. Unfortunately, their usefulness is limited because the reports of the various services are not comparable.

In all these off-duty programs, as in the larger total adult- and

[7] Ralph J. Klein, "The University of Maryland's Overseas Program," *Adult Education*, 10:2 (Winter 1960), 90–100.

university-extension education effort, American colleges and universities are developing a variety of programs to meet the growing needs of adults for continuing education. They are relying less and less on the more traditional procedures in such matters as rigid resident requirements, and are increasingly relying on a more flexible system of credit by examination and a combination of home study with shorter periods of residence on the campus.

Education of Dependents

A description of education in the Armed Forces would be incomplete without some attention given to those situations in which the services operate and administer elementary and secondary schools for their own children. In March 1963 2,391,532 children were military dependents.[8] Most of these dependents who were of school age attended institutions in the United States along with the children of the civilian population. However, under two sets of circumstances some of these dependents attend schools under the administration of military authorities located on military installations in the United States or overseas.

Section 6 of Public Law 874, enacted September 30, 1950, requires the U.S. Commissioner of Education to arrange for the education of children residing on federal property if, after he has consulted with the appropriate State educational agency, in his judgment no local educational agency is able to provide "suitable free public education" for these children. On March 30, 1962, the Secretary of Health, Education, and Welfare announced that local public elementary and secondary education which was provided on a racially segregated basis was not suitable free public education.[9] Information furnished by the Department of Defense in September 1964 indicated that, under the authority of Section 6 of Public Law 874 the military departments were operating 23 dependent schools, six of which offered instruction through the twelfth grade.

There were 38,282 pupils and 1742 teachers and other school

---

[8] *Department of Defense Annual Report for Fiscal Year 1963* (Washington, D.C.: USGPO, 1964), p. 335.

[9] Memorandum, dated February 8, 1963, to the Secretary of the Army, Secretary of the Navy, Secretary of the Air Force, from the Bureau of Educational Assistance Programs, Office of Education, Department of Health, Education, and Welfare.

officials in these schools. The operating cost in 1964 was $16,-749,416, including salaries, transportation, supplies, equipment, and instructional materials. The instructional staff was composed of civilian teachers who met the certification standards, and who were paid the salaries that prevailed in the area in which the military installations were located.[10]

The second circumstance under which the military operate and administer dependent schools is brought about by the deployment overseas of some 700,000 military personnel. In many instances, and where conditions permit, the serviceman is accompanied by his family. In December 1963, 291 service-operated dependent schools were located in 28 countries, with a student load of about 155,000 and with approximately 6,000 civilian teachers.[11] Authority to maintain and operate these schools is given in Public Law 86-91.

Through 1963 each of the military departments tended to operate and administer its overseas dependent schools with little coordination with the other services or with the Department of Defense. This gave rise to criticisms by individual teachers in the dependent schools and by such organizations as the Overseas Education Association and the National Education Association—dissatisfactions related to educational procedures, personnel actions, and salary matters. Because of these criticisms, Congress began to take a special interest in the operation and financing of these schools and instructed the Department of Defense to study the problem and take appropriate action.[12]

DOD brought this to the attention of the Defense Advisory Committee on Education. A survey committee of civilian educators was appointed and made its report in December 1962.[13]

The directive growing out of this report provides for a dependents school system operated by the military departments under the policy

---

[10] In contrast to practice in U.S. Armed Forces the British Army contains a separate Corps of school men and women in uniform. A.C.T. White, *The Story of Army Education, 1643–1963* (London: George G. Harrap & Co. Ltd.)

[11] *Department of Defense Appropriations for 1965: Part 2,* Hearings before a Subcommittee of the House Committee on Appropriations, 88th Congress, 2nd Session, p. 634.

[12] *Department of Defense Appropriations for 1963: Part 6,* Hearings before a Subcommittee of the House Committee on Appropriations, 87th Congress, 2nd Session, p. 61ff.

[13] *Overseas Dependents Schools: Recommendations for Improvement,* Report of Survey Committee appointed by Deputy Assistant Secretary of Defense (Education), Washington, D.C., December, 1962.

direction of the Assistant Secretary of Defense (Manpower), for the minor dependents of military and civilian personnel stationed overseas.[14]

The directive provides that:

A. The Assistant Secretary of Defense (Manpower) will
   1. Determine the general educational goals and objectives of the overseas dependent schools.
   2. Develop, in consultation with the U.S. Office of Education, appropriate curricula and lists of approved source materials for use in the schools.
   3. Provide for the procurement and distribution of school textbooks, workbooks, and other instructional materials, not normally available from military sources.
   4. Establish professional standards for all school professional personnel.
   5. Establish policies for common recruitment, selection, assignment, and transfer of all professional personnel.
   6. Develop standards for the operation and administration of the academic program.
B. The secretaries of the military departments will operate overseas dependents schools which are established on their installations. They will program, budget, and fund for all personnel and logistical support.
C. The secretaries of the military departments are assigned responsibility for academic administration of all dependents schools in the following areas:
   1. *Secretary of the Army*—European area, plus schools located in Turkey, Crete, Libya, Morocco, Ethiopia, and Pakistan.
   2. *Secretary of the Navy*—Atlantic school area.
   3. *Secretary of the Air Force*—Pacific school area.

The overseas dependents school system contemplated in the DOD directive went into effect on July 1, 1964. The estimated total operating cost of the system for fiscal year 1964 was $67,839,113.[15]

---

14 "Overseas Dependents Schools," Department of Defense Directive, Number 1342.6 (January 3, 1964).

15 *Department of Defense Annual Appropriations for 1965, op. cit.*, p. 646.

CHAPTER VII

Problem Areas

Like as a wise man in time of peace prepares for war.
Horace, *Satires, Book* II (65–68 BC)

Introduction

In keeping with the primary purpose of this monograph—to indicate the dimensions of the military training and educational task and to identify the various categories of the task—no attempt has been made to evaluate the programs or to make judgments on the manner in which they have been organized and conducted. This task is perhaps best left to future historians, who will be in a better position to judge the effectiveness of the Armed Forces in deterring war or in conducting such operations as are necessary for the furthering of national objectives. Certainly the efforts of all the Armed Forces (particularly since World War I) in organizing and training millions of men from a society which is decidedly unmilitaristic cannot be regarded as unsuccessful. Although other nations at various times may have developed superior tactics and special military skills, it is doubtful that any have surpassed the United States in the over-all development and employment of force in such a wide variety of circumstances as have occurred since the beginning of World War II. The extent to which this success can be attributed to the education and training programs of the Armed Forces can only be surmised. It is safe to conclude, however, that the part these programs have played has been significant.

Although this volume does not offer any evaluation of education in the Armed Forces, the student who wishes to study this area of educational activity will find extensive material in the proceedings of the various boards of senior officers that are convened periodically by each of the services. At various levels within the services there are statutory and other types of civilian boards and committees representing education, science, and industry.

The Defense Advisory Committee on Education in the Armed Services, the Commission on Accreditation of Service Experiences, the ROTC Advisory Committees, and the functions performed by the various regional accreditation associations have already been identified. Within each service, as well as in the Department of Defense, staff agencies—composed of both officers and civilians—devote their full time to the supervision and improvement of the various programs.[1] At times civilian consultants in the field of education are asked by the services to conduct surveys and analyses of military educational programs.[2] Students in the field of education who wish to make a contribution to their profession will find many areas needing further study and research in the important and extensive programs of education in the Armed Forces.

Education and Training Problems

The future success of the military training and education programs will depend in large part on how well certain problem areas are handled by those responsible for the programs. The problems in developing and conducting training and education programs are numerous and complex, and they are closely related to those faced by the services themselves. Most of them, however, fall within five main areas of concern.

Centralization of authority. First, there is an unmistakable and apparently irreversible trend toward greater unification of the separate services, with the concomitant centralization of decision-making at higher levels of authority. With the development of the so-called national defense agencies, which centralize common functions of the services, pressures inevitably will be brought to bear on the services to make greater use of common education and training facilities. A mistake that each of the services could make would be to ignore the reality of centralization and to continue costly training and education facilities that duplicate those of other services. On the other hand, the combination of education and training programs for the sake of centralization alone, both within and among the

---

[1] *Education Directory, 1963–64: Part 5,* "Federal Government" U.S. Office of Education (Washington, D.C.: USGPO, 1964).

[2] Ralph W. Tyler and Associates, *Analysis of the Purpose, Pattern, Scope, and Structure of the Officer Education Program of Air University,* Technical Memorandum 55-6 (Maxwell Air Force Base, Ala.: Officer Education Research Laboratory, May 1955), p. 260.

services, could lead to sterile and inflexible programs which fail to meet the specific requirements of any service.

Determining requirements. A second problem area is that of identifying requirements for training and education through systematic procedures that inspire confidence in their validity. With the increasing cost of weapon systems, those organizations responsible for training and education will probably find it even more difficult than in the past to compete with other service organizations for the limited manpower and dollar resources made available for defense purposes. Decisions on where money will be spent and for what specific purpose will come more and more to be made on the basis of the amount of defense that can be procured for the dollar expenditures. Unfortunately, it is difficult in many instances to cost out training, and particularly education, and to demonstrate the extent to which they contribute to the over-all defense effort.

In recent years, several of the services have taken steps to improve methods of determining training requirements for the operation and maintenance of new weapon systems before they come into the service inventory. Plans for the types of training and the numbers of personnel to be trained are made at the same time the research development leading to the procurement of the new weapon system is planned. The estimated cost of such training is often included in the estimated cost of the entire weapon system. In the more difficult area of education, the Air Force has established a standing committee known as the Educational Requirements Board. This unit is responsible for determining present and future requirements for various levels of officer education, within each of the occupational specialties as well as for professional military education.

Although improvements are being made in establishing valid requirements, the services might simplify the problem of obtaining support for education and training programs by providing clearer, more meaningful reports to the Department of Defense and the Congress. In examining the Annual Report of the Department of Defense,[3] one is struck by the relatively small amount of information on education and training, compared to the information on other areas of activity, such as research and development, supply, transportation, and personnel. The annual reports of the separate services

---

[3] *Department of Defense Annual Report: Fiscal Year 1962* (Washington, D.C.: USGPO, 1963), p. 430.

to the Defense Advisory Committee on Education in the Armed Services are worthwhile and extensive, but they tend to be confusing because the information presented by one service cannot readily be compared to that of another. Testimony before congressional committees often reveals a wide and unexplained variation in the reported costs for similar training and education programs among the services. This is perhaps more a function of the questions asked by the Congress than that of inadequate reports submitted by the services and by the Department of Defense. This need for more effective reporting procedures was highlighted by a congressional subcommittee in its study of the federal government and education in which the Department of Defense plays an important part.

> One of the reasons for a good deal of the confusion in all debate on the government's role in education is the inadequacy and misleading nature of educational statistics. In the first place, they are far from current. A second problem with educational statistics is that they include what each agency itself determines to be *education* and figures which each agency determines to be applicable. In many of the larger agencies there is not even, at a central point, complete knowledge of all the education programs they administer.[4]

Recognizing individual differences. A third problem area is concerned with the requirement to develop more flexible education and training programs. The Armed Forces have always been quick to use new instructional techniques and in many instances played an important part in their development. Widespread use of motion pictures, television, teaching machines, and ingenious simulators has been particularly noteworthy. However, in their instructional methods and curriculums the military have tended not to recognize the individual differences which exist within a group selected for training. From the most basic training courses to the senior professional military schools, the instructional programs are so highly standardized that all students in programs regardless of their abilities and previous training traditionally receive exactly the same instruction. The use of testing devices to identify individual differences among students and greater flexibility in curriculums to provide for them is clearly indicated especially in the higher levels of training and professional military education.

---

[4] *The Federal Government and Education,* H. R. Document No. 159. Presented by Mrs. Edith Green, Chairman of Special Subcommittee of the House Committee on Education and Labor (Washington, D.C.: USGPO, 1963), p. iv.

Retention of personnel.   A fourth problem area facing military education and training programs is directly related to the broader problems of the services. As the threat of general war subsides and the continuously expanding economy provides more career opportunities in the civilian community, the services will experience greater difficulty in recruiting and retaining highly qualified personnel for military careers. The problem may become more acute if the draft is discontinued—a possibility now under consideration by DOD. The training and education programs can and are doing a great deal to motivate personnel toward careers in the military. The services, however, will need to continue their efforts toward developing selection and assignment procedures to insure that highly trained individuals are given adequate opportunity to practice their skills and to enjoy the rewards ordinarily expected for achievement in any of the vocations and professions.

The problem of career progression in the officer corps is especially difficult. It is particularly difficult for the officer who becomes a highly trained specialist in the early stages of his career and later, as he progresses through the rank structure, is expected to assume broader responsibilities at higher levels. Here the professional military schools play an important part in preparing the specialist for the more general tasks of the military manager. But the officer who has been highly successful as a pilot, submariner, or infantry-platoon leader, may not necessarily be the best qualified to assume higher levels of command and staff responsibility. This complicates not only the problem of selection of the most qualified officer for the professional military schools but also the problem of creating realistic and worthwhile career plans for both the specialist and the general-duty officer.

An additional personnel problem is that of developing highly qualified staffs to manage and instruct in the education and training programs. In nearly all the institutions operated by the services, the faculties are made up of personnel whose primary careers are in areas other than education and training. Often they are recent graduates of the courses in which they are teaching. None of the services provides career opportunities for significant numbers of officers to become recognized scholars and teachers in various aspects of their own profession. This subject does not seem to be given adequate treatment in the various professional journals of the Armed Forces.

Educational lag. Finally, the military education and training programs are faced with the task of making effective contributions to the advancement of military art and science and of avoiding an educational and training lag behind technological advancement. All too often in the past these programs have been preoccupied, as have the services themselves, with current weapon systems, tactics, and strategies. Even more important, it will be essential that the pitfalls of overcommitment to a given weapon system, tactic, or strategy be avoided. It is quite probable that the degree of success to be achieved by these programs in the future will largely depend upon their ability to adjust to a rapidly changing world.

Bibliography

PUBLIC DOCUMENTS

Air University Library Index to Military Periodicals. Maxwell Air Force Base, Ala.: Air University Library.

Code of Federal Regulations, Title 33, Chap. I; Title 46, Chap. I.

Department of Defense Appropriations for 1964. Hearings before a Subcommittee of the House Committee on Appropriations, 88th Congress, 1st Session.

Department of Defense Appropriations for 1964, Hearings before the Subcommittee of the Senate Committee on Appropriations, 88th Congress, 1st Session.

Department of Defense Annual Report FY 1962: Including the Reports of the Secretary of Defense, Secretary of the Army, Secretary of the Navy, and the Secretary of the Air Force.

Education Directory, 1963–64: Part 5, "Federal Government," Department of Health, Education, and Welfare. U.S. Office of Education.

Hearings on Military Posture, 1964, before the House Committee on Armed Services, 88th Congress, 1st Session.

The Federal Government and Education, H. R. Document No. 159, presented by Mrs. Edith Green, Chairman of the Special Subcommittee of the House Committee on Education and Labor, 88th Congress, 1st Session.

Title 10, *United States Code.*

"United States Coast Guard," *Annual Report of the Department of the Treasury on the State of the Finances, For the Fiscal Year ended June 30, 1962,* pp. 185–95.

United States Government Organization Manual, 1963–64. Washington, D.C.: USGPO, June 1, 1963.

BOOKS

Clark, Harold F. and Harold S. Sloan, *Classrooms in the Military.* New York: Teachers College, Bureau of Publications, Columbia University, 1964, p. 154.

Foot, M. D. R., *Men in Uniform.* London: Weidenfeld and Nicholson, 1961, p. 163.

Hittle, J. D., *The Military Staff: Its History and Development.* Harrisburg, Pa.: The Stackpole Company, 1961, p. 286.

Huntington, Samuel P., *The Soldier and the State*. Cambridge, Mass.: Belknap Press, 1957, p. 534.

Janowitz, Morris, *The Professional Soldier*. New York: The Free Press of Glencoe, Inc., 1960, p. 464.

Lyons, Gene M. and John W. Masland, *Education and Military Leadership: A Study of the ROTC*. Princeton, N.J.: Princeton University Press, 1959, p. 283.

Masland, John W. and L. I. Radway, *Soldiers and Scholars*. Princeton, N.J.: Princeton University Press, 1957, p. 530.

Index

116 INDEX